DAKTARI

A Surgeon's Adventures
with the Flying Doctors of East Africa

DAKTARI

A Surgeon's Adventures
with the Flying Doctors of East Africa

by Thomas D. Rees, M.D.

SUNSTONE
PRESS
SANTA FE

Sunstone books may be purchased for educational, business, or sales promotional use. For information please write: Special Markets Department, Sunstone Press, P.O. Box 2321, Santa Fe, New Mexico 87504-2321.

FIRST EDITION

1 3 5 7 9 10 8 6 4 2

Library of Congress Cataloging-in-Publication Data:

Rees, Thomas D.
    Daktari: a surgeon's adventures with the flying doctors of East Africa / by Thomas D. Rees.
        p. cm.
    ISBN: 0-86534-366-7
        1. Rees, Thomas D. 2. Surgeons—Africa, East—Biography. 3. Plastic surgeons—Africa, East—Biography. 4. Aeronautics in medicine—Africa, East. I. Title.

RD27.35 R437 A3 2002
617'.092—dc21
[B]   2002036486

SUNSTONE PRESS
Post Office Box 2321
Santa Fe, NM 87504-2321 / USA
(505) 988-4418 / orders only (800) 243-5644
FAX (505) 988-1025
www.sunstonepress.com

Published in

This book is dedicated to the women of AMREF
and the Flying Doctors of Africa

Sue (Shu Shu), Nan, Connie, Leonora, Anne, and Nicky.
Without their support, the Flying Doctors
would not have happened.

"It is better to light a single candle
than to curse the darkness"

—Albert Shweitzer

ACKNOWLEDGMENTS

There are literally hundreds of individuals who have contributed their time, energy, expertise, money, and support to the Flying Doctors of East Africa since it's inception in 1956. Many have served and are serving now as members of the Boards of Directors of the African Medical and Research Foundation (AMREF) in Africa, as well as the national country offices in the US, Canada. Great Britain, Sweden, Italy, Germany, France, Denmark, Austria, Holland, Spain, and Monaco. Many others have toiled on the front lines of the Flying Doctors in Africa: pilots, doctors, nurses, health care workers, laboratory technicians, anesthetists, educators, researchers, clerks, secretaries, drivers, mechanics, radio technicians, team leaders, program directors, country leaders and coordinators in the various national offices in the African countries served by AMREF including Kenya, Uganda, Tanzania, Somalia, Ethiopia, Mozambique, Zanzibar, South Africa, Sudan, Ethiopia and Rwanda

The following people, both deceased and living, are some who have contributed to the development and growth of the Flying Doctors over these many years. I owe them a heartfelt thanks for their unswerving efforts, devotion, and steadfast loyalty to our cause through the many ups and downs of the organization as we struggled for viability and success in reaching our goal of improving the health care of Africans.

My initial thanks goes to my cofounders, Sir Archibald McIndoe and Sir Michael Wood, both of whom are deceased. I owe an enormous debt of gratitude to the late Ron Moss who since the very beginning has devoted countless hours and unlimited energy to the success of the Flying Doctors both in America, Europe, and Africa. My special thanks also to Leonora Semler of Germany, Nicky Blundell-Brown and Lady Susan

Wood of Kenya, the late Dr. Anne Spoerry of Kenya, and my wife Nan who have served AMREF so well. They can never be adequately rewarded for their devotion.

I am indebted to Kenneth Ross for his editorial help. He finally managed to steer me away from the passive voice. And to Graeme Backhurst for scrupulously checking the final manuscript for accuracy of dates, times, places, events and people, and for crossing t's and dotting i's. Ms Amy Bookman helped arrange the material in a more logical sequence, and Nicky Blundell-Brown did a final accuracy check on details.

I thank: Dr. Peter Papworth, Dr. Erik Nordberg, Sir Miles Clifford, Sue Pretzlik, Dr. Mike Gerber, Dr. Chris Wood, Dr. Bill Adams-Ray, Dr. Donald Gilchrist, Bill Bunford, Mervyn Cowie, Pauline Ravn, Musa Amalemna, Paul Nones, Jim Heather-Hayes, Maggie Maina, Danielli Lomoni, Sister Winifred Robinson, Sister Rosemary Sandercock, Dr. Jimmie James, Dr. Tom Raassen, Bethuel Kiplagat, Simeon Shitemi, Dr. Peter Ngatia, Dr Vinand Nantulya, Dr. Pat Youri, Margaret Mudeshi, Dr. Eunice Kiereini, Dr. John Wachira, Doris Block, Roy Kirkpatrick, Marie Marsh, Greta Rowe, Jeff Baker, Dr. William Burkitt, Ambrose Appelbe, Harvey Picker, Dr. Marc Wood, Bill Davis, Joe Moran, Jim Noone, Jackie Cochrane, Tommy Lanphier, Dr, Hale Tolleth, Dr.Charles Ramsden, Dr. Robert Hicks, Dr. Steve Miller, Dr. Ralph Bowen, Dr. Lawrence Birnbaum, Dr. Wilson Kerr, Dr. Elliot Berg, Dr. Richard Kostecki, Dr. Hugo Keunen, Rozlyn Sherrif, Phil Mathews, Dave Allen, Hilary Prendergast, Elizabeth Long, Hugh De Glanville, Dunston Omari, John Storey, Malin Sorsbie, Lord Arthur Porrit, Michel Gwebwe, Isabel Mbugua, Dr. David Furnas, Dr. Marlene Long, Dr. Osman Mustafa, Alan Holmes, Meshak Ndisi, Dr. Roy Shaffer, Lady Constance McIndoe, Dr. David Brooke, Maddie DeMott, Bruce Bodner, Charles Garner, Ned Bandler, Don Rice, Fay Harbach, K.C. Fuller, James Niven, Prof. J. M. Kyambi, Amy Bookman, Francine Leinhardt, Ann Kent Taylor, Geoffrey Kent, Bill Bernhard. Priscilla Goldfarb, Dr. Alfonso Villalonga, Dr. Jane Carter, Dr. Bettina Vadera, Grace Kimuyu, Joanne Wood, Nancy Maksud, Isabel Mbugua, Elizabeth Githachuri, Dr. Jane Wright, Dr. George Brown, Bob Lilley, Bob Fairchild, Jack Block, Dr. Michael Alderman, Sylvia Mudasia, Dr. Festus Ilako, Judy Fehlig, Nancy Hutson, Craig Saxton, Gerry Byrne, Dr. Sam Basch, Peter Buttenweiser, Amb. Alan Blinken, Bill Collison, Kristen Conor, Countess Albina Du Boisvrouvray, Allan Grossman, Dr. David Niamaya, Mette Kjaer, Dr. Joe Kennedy, Leo Kelmenson, Phyllis Sheridan, Dr. Javier Beut, Anthony Marshal, Jim Sheffield, George Van Der Ploeg, Dwight Wait, Jim Monroe, Karen Cassard, Bella Ocholla, Peter Flanigan, Hans Tuyt, Tommy Simmons, Constance van Haeften,

Ilaria Borletti, Seana Massey, Dennis White, Dr. Basil King, Winfried Zacher, Bo Karlstrom, Kristina Kuylenstierna, Vera Axelson Johnson, Helena Bonnier, Fran Howard, Alistair Boyd, Alexander Heroys, Bettie Throne-Holst, Dr. John Evans, Bridget Lawson, John Nixon, John Patterson, Scott Grifflin, Alan Torie, Arthur Godfrey, Bob Redford, Paul Newman, Walter Cronkhite, Kirk Douglas, Johnnie Carson, Mr. and Mrs. Julius Heldman, Mr. and Mrs. Ted Stanley, Barbara Windom, Dave Grusin, and Ted Flicker. And special thanks to my great friend Jonathan Kenworthy, the world renowned artist, who generously lent his special talents in support of AMREF on several occasions.

Many names of people who have served AMREF and the Flying Doctors so well over the years do not appear here who should. The fault is mine because of my increasingly fuzzy memory and because many records are missing for which I sincerely apologize. I hope I will be forgiven.

INTRODUCTION

It is impossible in one volume to chronicle the history of the Flying Doctors of Africa from its beginning in 1956 until the present. Indeed, such was not my purpose in writing this book; rather, I have written about a few adventures in which I was a participant, neglecting hundreds of stories, in which I was not. The narrative is not continuous, but the stories are pretty much in chronological order. A detailed history of the Flying Doctors would fill several volumes and will, I hope, be written by others.

Since its beginning, many colorful and larger-than-life people have been involved with the Flying Doctors of Africa. I wish I could do justice to each. I am forever grateful for their support and friendship over these many years. Each has added a rich dimension to my life. Many are still actively at work with AMREF, the parent organization of the Flying Doctors, others have retired and, sadly, others have passed on. Sir Archibald McIndoe, one of the three founders of the Flying Doctors, died in 1960 shortly after we began our work. Sir Michael Wood died in 1987, leaving me as the last remaining member of our trio of founders.

To avoid confusion, the reader should know at the outset that throughout this book the acronym AMREF (the African Medical and Research Foundation) is used interchangeably with the Flying Doctors of Africa. The Flying Doctors of Africa is a division of AMREF and is known throughout the Western World for its work in rescue, emergency situations, and for providing specialty surgical and medical care throughout East Africa. The parent organization AMREF is widely recognized as a leader in the delivery of health care systems to the rural and urban poor of Sub-Saharan Africa, and especially for its educational and training programs.

A fortuitous set of circumstances first took me to Africa in 1956. It has been more than four decades since that first trip. Much has happened in the intervening years. I went back to Africa time and again. I still go there. Along with Archie and Mike I started the Flying Doctors of East Africa. What began with three surgeons and a small Piper Tripacer airplane grew into the largest non-governmental health care organization in Africa, with a permanent staff of over five hundred, a fleet of airplanes, an extensive radio network, and a responsibility to bring health care, public health and educational services to hundreds of thousands of Africans.

This book recalls a few of the adventures I shared with Archie, Mike and others while working with the Flying Doctors. The stories are all true. Many of the people in them are still living but sadly, others are gone. I have used real names whenever possible, but sometimes resorted to pseudonyms where individuals can no longer be located or where the telling may cause discomfort. The surgical operations described all took place, but not, for the sake of organization, and to avoid unnecessary repetitions, at the hospitals cited in the text. After more than forty years in operation, there are literally hundreds of amazing stories of the Flying Doctors—stories of war, natural disasters, epidemics, car, train, and plane accidents, daring night rescues from unlit landing strips, tales of personal bravery and sacrifice. I only wish I could narrate all of them here.

Recently, I discussed with my son the dilemma of how to begin this book. He reminded me of a note I had scribbled on the title page of a textbook I had given him as a gift. It said in part "Where have all those years gone?" That is my feeling exactly when I look back on the experiences I have had in Africa. They are vivid in my mind, despite the passage of time.

Aging has its gifts, and one of them is the revivification of memory, not short-term memory, but memories of the past. There is pleasure in the telling of stories, the sharing of adventures and the pursuit of meaning. I offer these stories to you, the reader, in the hope that they will inspire in you the courage to seek your own destiny and the desire, as Joseph Campbell has put it, to find your bliss.

1

The Adventures Begin

On a table in a rustic farmhouse on the slopes of Mount Kilimanjaro a Maasai *moran* (warrior) lay on his back, quite still, teeth clenched, his handsome Nilotic face stoic but betraying pain. From an ugly rent in his belly dark blood slowly oozed, flowing down over the sides of his body and dripping to form a dark red puddle on the table beneath him. A filthy ochre-red blanket was wrapped tightly around his body in a desperate effort to stem the bleeding and hold his guts in place inside his abdomen; the blanket now lay partially open, revealing the wound. I could see the unmistakable glisten of intestinal loops bulging through the hole in his abdominal wall.

A few hours before, while driving his cattle herd to water, he had surprised a rhinoceros foraging in thick bush. Alarmed at this intrusion into his space, the enormous beast charged, impaling the Maasai with his massive horn. The attack lasted only seconds but the horn, a formidable weapon, had torn through his groin and pierced his abdominal cavity. Tossing him aside like a rag doll, the animal trotted away and left the man to die. But he did not die and if I could overcome the gnawing insecurity that wrenched my own gut, he would not die now. I had never seen such a devastating wound in all of my experience in the emergency rooms of the various hospitals in which I had trained, and the clinical detachment, which all surgeons learn to rely on, temporarily vanished.

I was young and self confident but my surgical training had been in modern hospitals with state-of-the-art equipment and technology. I knew that never again in my career would I be more knowledgeable, even though my skills would be continuously honed over the next few decades. In the United States such a problem would be difficult and serious, but with every chance of success if dealt with promptly and skillfully. Here in the bush, many miles from any medical facility, with night coming on, I was apprehensive and feeling very insecure, stripped of all the back-ups that I was accustomed to. How was I going to save this man's life without the support systems that I was accustomed to; without IV fluids, blood for transfusion, adequate anesthesia and with only rudimentary instruments?

The series of events that led to this predicament began in London on a cold blustery day, in January of 1956. I was having lunch with my then teacher and mentor, Sir Archibald McIndoe, whom I had met while on a surgical tour of Europe. I had been lucky enough to be immersed in a postgraduate fellowship in plastic surgery with this extraordinary man. The opportunity to study under McIndoe was sought by many young surgeons and granted only to a lucky few. I was the first American to be appointed to this coveted fellowship, established by the Marks family of England. I came by the appointment fortuitously; that intangible element of fate or karma. It was the chance of a lifetime and I eagerly took it.

Sir Archibald—Archie to his friends—was arguably the most famous plastic surgeon in the world in the post-World War II era. His reputation was earned as Chief Surgeon to the RAF during and after the war. Archie had formed a prestigious plastic surgery unit at the Queen Victoria Hospital in East Grinstead, England, in what had formerly been a small country hospital. During World War II and after, he had recruited a crack team of promising young surgeons; those who showed the most promise of becoming experts in the nascent field of reconstructive surgery. East Grinstead treated hundreds of young RAF pilots, the men who were England's most revered war heroes. The aerial war they fought in their Spitfire and Hurricane airplanes had surely saved England from German invasion and the rehabilitation of their injured pilots was a national priority.

During World War II a typical airman's injury was a deep burning of the face and hands, incurred when flames and hot gases scorched the cockpit when the plane was hit by enemy shellfire—Archie likened such burns to those being caused by a "blow torch" in that they were caused by intense heat being delivered in a very short period of time. Survivors were most often Hurricane pilots. Most Spitfire pilots perished because the two fuel tanks were located in front of the pilots, one above the other. Unless the pilot could eject almost instantly, the explosions of superheated gasoline quickly incinerated him. The Hurricane pilot had a slightly better chance of living because the main fuel tanks were in the wings, with a reserve tank behind the instrument panel. The reserve tank often blew up after a wing tank had caught fire.

A pilot's burns were usually inflicted in the last few moments before he could parachute from his airplane. The face and hands were primarily involved because of the pilot's immediate and subconscious reaction to the flame was to remove his goggles and gloves. The thick whole-body flying suits of the time usually saved him from more extensive burning. Many inventive techniques in reconstructive surgery were developed by McIndoe and his staff in response to the injuries of the RAF pilots. As a result, many operations of skin grafting and reconstructive surgery over a period of many months were usually required in the more severely burned men to restore a semblance of normal appearance and function for their crippled hands and fingers. Archie was recognized as an innovator by plastic surgeons all over the world—especially the young ones of my generation. He was a public hero in England because of his identification with the courageous fighter pilots and he was awarded a knighthood for his pioneering work by a grateful King.

McIndoe had a physical presence befitting his fame. He was physically imposing with a stocky, muscular build and prominent facial features. He lacked perfect Grecian proportions but was handsome in a rugged way; a sort of man's man. His hands were large, with thick strong fingers, not those ordinarily associated with the delicate work required of a plastic surgeon. There was nothing dainty about him. He was tough, persistent, demanding and would never let go of an idea if he thought he was right. He could also be stubborn and at times unreasonable. Archie could get things done by the sheer force of his personality, which rubbed people up the wrong way on occasion. Nevertheless, he was recognized by all who saw him operate as one of the greatest surgical technicians of his time.

Archie was endowed with enormous charm and charisma and his intense magnetism and wit were irresistible. He was adept at using the force of his personality to achieve practical goals, a quality which later proved to be very useful when we formed the Flying Doctors of Africa. He associated with rich and powerful people all over the world but never for reasons of snobbery or class affiliation. Archie never lost sight of his goals, which were altruistic and deeply felt. He was a superb money raiser, for example. When Archie asked people for help they could see the depth of his passion and responded with generosity. He was a man with a big soul, and people knew it. His prodigious gifts were never private possessions, they belonged in a sense to the whole world, and he spent much of his life giving those gifts away.

Archie became addicted to traveling to East Africa each year to escape the damp, cold English winter and to renew his energy with the healing powers of the

African sun. He delighted in tromping around his farm in Tanganyika (since renamed Tanzania) in a pair of khaki shorts and desert boots. In England even God was civilized, but in Africa spirituality was primal; a place where the gods were capricious and unpredictable. It was a wide space where you could feel more and think less. In Africa it was quiet enough to hear your inner voice. In England everyday life was highly regimented and the natural world largely domesticated. In Africa life was spontaneous and unpredictable, and nature was still wild. Consequently, Africa was a strong source of spiritual healing for Archie. As with many others who were afflicted with urban and secular malaise, Archie found solace in the brilliant light, rolling savannahs and ancient mountains of Africa.

Archie was deeply concerned about the welfare of people, and not just their surgical problems. He recognized that the repair of disfiguring wounds was only the first step in returning a person to a normal life. The second step was to heal the soul, the inner person. This combination of traits made Archie more than a great surgeon, he was a great man and I was immediately and immensely attracted to him. In fact, I was overwhelmed by his presence. When he offered me a job as his personal assistant and Marks Fellow, it was one of the happiest days of my life. My presence here, at this place, was due entirely to his influence. And the fate of the Maasai man before me was somehow related to a confluence of all the factors which had conspired to form my own destiny.

It was during my fellowship with Archie that I met another physician named Michael Wood. Mike and I immediately became fast friends, a friendship that lasted until his death. Mike practiced as a general surgeon in Kenya after World War II. In his practice he was confronted daily with disfigured patients, particularly children, who desperately needed specialized surgical skills—skills he lacked. Archie, on his annual pilgrimages to East Africa, would often help out, teaching Mike with every patient they treated. There were no surgeons trained in plastic surgery at that time in the whole of East Africa. Mike was so challenged by this need that he took a sabbatical from his practice in Kenya and returned to England in 1955 to obtain formal training in plastic and reconstructive surgery, under the tutelage of his friend, Archie McIndoe.

Mike had originally emigrated to Africa because he suffered from bronchial asthma and believed that his condition would be improved in a warm, sunny climate. Soon after his arrival in Kenya, Mike established a thriving general surgery practice. His skill, easy manner and caring attitude made him an immediate success and his schedule and waiting room filled. He fitted easily into the society of fiercely independent expatriates who had come to reside in East Africa. Contrary to most of his white countrymen, however, he and his wife became champions of black African rights and worked for franchising the black vote through his active support of the Capricorn Africa Society. For this he was suspect in some white circles.

Mike was ruggedly handsome; over six feet tall, with the slight barrel chest and hunched shoulders of an asthmatic. He had a Gary Cooper kind of appeal. His hair was light brown, which he combed straight back, but it rarely stayed. A few stray wisps always found their way over his ears and forehead, which along with his slightly askew tie and escaped shirt tail, conveyed a dignified if somewhat disheveled impression. His eyes were intensely turquoise blue and penetrating. Laugh lines radiated from the corners, betraying his ready smile and good sense of humor and magnified by a skin constantly tanned from an outdoor life and flying. Mike shared many of Archie's best attributes. Like him, he was utterly appealing and had great charisma. He immediately put at ease all whom he met. He exuded confidence, and his manner was particularly soothing to patients suffering from pain or fear. He also had an enigmatic quality that was immensely appealing. He was a complex man of considerable depth and people could sense it.

Mike's life in East Africa provided a continuous series of challenges and adventures, each of which he met with relish. He was a surgeon, pilot, farmer, human rights activist, family man, social reformer and above all, a humanitarian. He had a restless spirit, boundless energy and an inquisitive mind. His continuous battle with asthma only strengthened his resolve to meet life's challenges and conquer them. He possessed an easy-going disposition, even when sorely tried. During the many years I knew him, and in the many adventures we shared, I never saw him lose his composure in the operating room or public life. He seemed capable of overcoming any obstacle with a steady persistence.

Men admired Mike because of his lack of concern for the common ambitions of modern urban life. He did not lust after money or the career goals that seem so important to most of us. The accumulation of material possessions was not important to him. He was in love with adventure, and had great fun doing such things as racing Porsches (although he did not own one) in the famous East African Safari Rally. And, of course, he was in love with airplanes. But it was not the possession of airplanes or rally cars that he craved, it was the thrill of flying and racing that attracted him.

Archie and Mike shared an immense passion for Africa. Archie would always talk about his yearly visits with great enthusiasm. With considerable emotion, he often described to me the love of his life, a vast wheat farm in the foothills of Kilimanjaro, a farm that Archie and Robin Johnson (an ex RAF ace and former patient) literally built from the raw bush. The land had over a thousand acres of wheat under cultivation and employed more than three hundred Africans.

One day in London in 1956, I had lunch with Archie. He was going to leave for his annual visit to Africa the following week. Much to my surprise he asked me if I would like to go with him. He said that I would not believe the number of interesting patients with surgical problems that we could see and operate on while there. It was the kind of experience I could never get in a residency in New York or London. We could also travel into the bush and see some of the country and its animals. Archie said that it was time to escape the beastly English winter and feel the warmth of the African sun. I did not need to be convinced; there was no question that I would accept his offer. Like so many others, I had read a great deal about Africa, especially the adventures of explorers and hunters. The idea of going to Kenya with this great man was overwhelmingly exciting. I accepted quickly, before Archie could change his mind. I knew that my wife, who had never wavered in her support of my ambition through my long years of surgical training, would approve.

Over lunch, Archie reminded me that Mike would just be starting his practice in Kenya as the first qualified plastic surgeon in an area much larger than Europe. His patient population would include people from the whole of East Africa—Kenya, Uganda and Tanganyika. It was incredible to imagine that he would be the only plastic surgeon in an area so vast. Archie thought that he and I could provide some moral support for Mike and help him embark on his plastic surgery career. There is more plastic surgery to do in Africa than we can do in a lifetime, he said. You will gain a rich experience that you will never forget. I knew he was right. And so it was, that on my very first sojourn in Africa I found myself confronted with this gravely injured but uncomplaining Maasai man. And it was with Archie and Mike that I would share the challenge and the adventure of saving his life.

Archie was a seasoned surgeon, accustomed to the pressures of emergency surgery. The broken and disfigured bodies of RAF pilots had been his stock-in-trade, and the random accidents and virulent pathologies of Africa were no stranger to him. I was more accustomed to the elective procedures and prearranged surgeries typical of an American or British hospital. Very little is left to chance in Western medicine and improvisation is discouraged in favor of tried-and-true protocols. This surgery was not elective or prearranged, and its outcome would depend almost entirely on our ability to improvise.

Archie's chief concern, of course, was for the patient; but his secondary concern was for my education—and it was clear that he expected me to take primary responsibility for treating the man who lay before us. Mike's job would be to get him to a hospital at daybreak. For this emergency his task was to be a pilot, not a surgeon. Mike was an hour's flight away and had been reached by radio. In Africa you have to be versatile and if someone's life depended more on your ability to fly an airplane than wield a scalpel, then that is what you did. In the days before global positioning satellites, flying by compass and dead reckoning over a trackless wilderness and landing on a dirt airstrip took considerable skill. Mike was up to it.

The Maasai *moran* had already lost a great deal of blood. Despite the severe wound, he had managed to walk several miles while holding his intestines in place with his old blanket. Eventually, he collapsed near his village (*manyatta*). From there his fellow tribesmen had carried him to the farm, bundled up in his bloody old blanket. It was a miracle that he had managed to walk at all, but his strength and stoicism were typical of the Maasai who, at that time, were still largely unaffected by Western civilization. His appearance communicated the cultural distance between us. His hair was plaited and covered with red ochre and mud, and his only clothing was a shawl of animal skin and the blood-soaked blanket. His earlobes were pierced and stretched so that they hung in long loops, into one of which he had inserted a can containing his supply of snuff. He was bleeding actively.

I carefully removed the blanket, exposing the terrible gash. On closer examination, it appeared that the wound was smeared with a mixture of mud and cow dung—according to Archie, a common practice amongst some of the Maasai, who believe such a mixture to be a potent medicine to ward off infection. This concerned me, because dung often contains tetanus spores and gas gangrene bacilli—both deadly infections. Of course, there was no tetanus vaccine available on the farm. Indeed, I had no blood, plasma, IV salt solutions, antibiotics, or general anesthesia. I did have several doses of morphine to help combat the shock and pain, a rudimentary medical kit with a scalpel and several hemostats, scissors, and forceps.

Despite these desperate circumstances, the patient was calm and not as deeply in shock as I would have expected from such a wound. He seemed fairly alert. His eyes were veiled with pain. The pale color of his tongue and the conjunctiva of his eyelids were tell-tale signs of significant blood loss and anemia. His pulse was fast and weak but steady; not the rapid, thready, racing pulse of deep shock. I had no instrument to measure his blood pressure, nor did I have a stethoscope. As we examined him, Archie and I struggled to contain the intestinal loops within the abdominal cavity. We fashioned a crude support by wrapping his abdomen snugly with torn strips of bed sheet until we could clean him up and operate.

I felt frustrated and helpless. After years of training, I was confident to tackle most surgical problems, but here I was miles from anywhere with few instruments and virtually none of the equipment that I had grown to rely on. I fought to conceal my indecision from Archie. I believe he sensed my anguish. I asked him, how can we treat this man? We had to do something to save him, and soon. If we could patch him together enough to get through the night, hopefully he would survive until Mike arrived in the morning. If not, he would most assuredly die before daybreak. After discussing the surgical options, Archie and I decided to perform the simplest possible surgery. We planned to remove any obviously gangrenous portion of both the large and small intestines, and exteriorize any large bowel that was damaged by the rhino horn so we could divert the fecal stream. Exteriorization involves moving any damaged or potentially nonviable portion of the intestine outside the abdomen. Leaving dead bowel tissue inside the abdominal cavity would result in rupture and peritonitis.

As we prepared to implement our plan, the terrible reality confronted us: we had no choice but to operate without general anesthesia. This was not quite as horrendous as it might seem, since the intestinal walls have few nerve fibers that convey pain, but the thought of it made me a little queasy. Not long ago all surgery was done without anesthesia, often to the accompaniment of the patient's agonized screams. In this case, most of the distress would be from the wound in the abdominal wall itself or from traction (pulling) on the intestines. But there would be pain, and it could be severe, further adding to shock. How would this man react? A couple of stiff belts of Scotch along with an injection of morphine provided some relief (for the patient, that is). Not the best treatment for shock, but it was all we had to offer.

The farmer, speaking Maasai, explained to the patient as best he could what we were going to do. He accepted the decision without question. He was amazingly aware of his surroundings considering the severity of his injury. Luckily, even under the influence of Scotch and morphine, his pulse remained steady and relatively strong, indicating that his shock had not worsened. Without blood and IV fluids, all we could do was wrap him in warm blankets and elevate his feet to improve the blood flow to his brain and vital organs.

While we boiled the instruments to sterilize them, I thoroughly scrubbed the skin of his body around the wound with ordinary bath soap and water, the only antiseptic available. As a further precaution, I painted the skin with vodka, taking care not to spill any inside the abdomen. It was a somewhat crude method of sterilization, but vodka is alcoholic. It was very difficult to contain his intestines inside the abdominal cavity during this preparation. Archie, using both hands, held the intestines in place as best he could with a clean sheet while I scrubbed the skin. After these simple preparations he was ready for surgery.

I thought about the treatment this man would have received at the New York Hospital-Cornell Medical Center where I trained, where he would have been surrounded by anesthesiologists, residents, interns, surgeons, nurses, medical students, and all of the technical apparatus and paraphernalia that attend such a serious emergency. Oxygen bottles, stomach tubes, intravenous bottles containing electrolyte fluid, anesthesia machines, monitoring equipment to track his EKG and oxygen saturation, intravenous antibiotics, and, of course, cross-matched blood standing by. But alas, none such was available to us.

Picking up the scalpel, still warm from the boiling water, I first removed the portion of small intestine that was obviously not viable, then sutured the healthy ends together to re-establish continuity of the intestinal tract. Next, I carefully brought the damaged section of the transverse colon out through the abdominal wound and stabilized it outside his abdomen with stitches to the skin. Having no proper suture material, I used ordinary silk thread from a sewing spool, a common suture material before the discovery of modern sutures such as Tevdek or Vicryl. We elected to postpone cutting away any part of the large bowel because we were unsure how much damage had been done by the rhino horn. We couldn't clearly determine where the compromised tissue ended and the healthy tissue began. We knew that the prudent option under such conditions is to exteriorize the bowel and wait to see how much is devitalized later, when it is more obvious.

In the meantime I cut a hole into the colon, emptied it, and sewed this temporary drain to the skin of his lower abdomen, providing a colostomy. A temporary colostomy minimizes the spillage of infectious feces into the abdominal cavity, thereby reducing the risk of peritonitis. Because of the contamination of the wound that had already occurred from the breached colon and cow dung, it was out of the question to sew the bowel together at that time. I decided to wait, knowing that if he survived, the colon could be repaired later when his condition improved. I repaired the abdomen by sewing the wound edges together around the improvised colostomy. We worked as fast as we could to reduce the trauma.

Throughout the procedure the patient was restless but uncomplaining. He did not vocalize the extent of his pain. He frequently took deep breaths but never seemed to lose consciousness, as far as I could determine. He spoke occasionally in a low voice, which of course I could not understand. His self control and fortitude were simply amazing. Somehow this man was able to remain composed in a situation that would reduce most westerners to hysteria. Even in the midst of his agony this brave Maasai possessed great dignity and an almost Zen-like calm.

After we had done all we could, Archie and I simply sat with him and kept vigil. Throughout the night we gave him sips of water to which we had added table salt and some baking soda to provide as much electrolyte replacement as we could without the benefit of intravenous solutions. We also added honey for energy. We kept him warm with blankets. In the stillness of the night we talked little, turning our thoughts inward, and prayed silently. I dispensed the remaining doses of morphine and a small amount of penicillin that we had left over from our recent surgical safari. The Maasai met the night with courage, retreating to some distant, comforting place, deep within his psyche. I wondered what he was thinking; if he was thinking. This strange man, in this vast mysterious place, was an enigma to me. He seemed to have inner resources no longer accessible to, or perhaps simply forgotten by, people of the West. It was a testimony to the power of his spirit that he had made it this far, but he could not last indefinitely. Our only hope now was to get him to a hospital as soon as possible where he could receive blood transfusions and IV fluids, intensive antibiotics and medication for pain.

About an hour after first light, we heard the drone of an approaching airplane. It was Mike. He made a low pass over the farm, checking the runway for obstruction, circled around and headed in. In a couple of minutes and to our great relief, he landed and taxied up the farm's dirt strip. The three of us moved the patient into the little Piper Tripacer as gently as possible. It was undoubtedly his first airplane ride, although he was in no condition to enjoy it. We gave Mike a briefing on the patient's condition and in a few moments he was off again, bumping along the rough airstrip as the little plane strained to get airborne. Quiet descended as he disappeared over the horizon. A great sense of relief came over me.

It must have been an exceedingly strange experience for this Maasai warrior, a man rooted in the natural world, to be suddenly thrust into the hands of Western doctors. For his illness was fate, not pathology, and traditional healers were practitioners of an art, not a technology. Yet there was art in what we had done too. And given the option, he did not choose blind faith, but sought the benefits, however incomprehensible, of Western medicine. How would this experience change him? Or would it? An hour later Mike would admit him to the government hospital at Arusha. There he would undergo more strange experiences. How would he integrate it all into his worldview?

As Archie and I walked back to the farmhouse from the airstrip, I wondered how this adventure would affect me. If I had helped to save a man's life, then he in turn had changed my own. I wasn't sure why, but I knew that my life's direction, somehow, had been permanently altered. This chance encounter with a stoic, dignified, Maasai man, in this enigmatic, faraway place had taken hold of me. I think Archie knew it would somehow happen.

2

Baptism of Fire

From the day that Archie invited me on our trip to Africa until the day three weeks later when we stood in line to board a BOAC Super Constellation at Heathrow airport, bound for Nairobi, I had been in a state of high anticipation. As a boy, like so many others, I had always been fascinated with Africa. I had read of the exploits of famous hunters and explorers like David Livingstone, Morton Stanley, Richard Francis Burton, John Speke, Carl Ackley, Jim Corbet, Andrew Selous, Teddy Roosevelt and just about everyone else who had written about their adventure in the "dark continent." The fictional exploits in the writings of Alan Quartermain had also been favorite reading. While waiting for our trip to begin, I eagerly consumed other books about Africa, its people, animals, and history. Everything I learned only increased my curiosity. As we climbed the stairs to the plane, Archie said that I was about to have an adventure and it would be unlike anything I had ever imagined. How prophetic he was. I was already intrigued with the mystique of Africa even before arriving there. My reading only whetted my appetite to visit this fascinating and mysterious continent.

Affording the trip was a major problem for me. My financial situation was bleak to say the least. I was earning the equivalent of three hundred dollars a month as a Fellow with Archie, not enough to even cover my airfare. Nan, my wife, continued her career as a fashion model in New York during my fellowship to keep us financially afloat as she had done during the previous five years of my surgical training. I loathed asking her to finance my journey. I felt a bit guilty as I thought the trip was more in the nature of a vacation than work, but of course she readily agreed that I should not miss such a unique opportunity to visit Africa with someone as knowledgeable as Sir Archibald.

The plane was tourist class only, with seats jammed together tightly on either side of a narrow aisle to accommodate the largest possible number of passengers. It was propeller driven, of course, so it would be slow and noisy. Old prop planes vibrated constantly, finding the resonant frequency of every object inside, including the people. As we lumbered down the runway and into the air for the long flight, the roar of the big piston engines and the changing harmonic of the props gradually settled into a loud, monotonous drone. The flight was going to be a prolonged assault on the senses. It was too noisy to talk comfortably and the cramped conditions made me want to pull inside myself. After a while, shielded by the wall of sound, I managed to retreat within, seeking some psychic privacy, and withdrew into a world of introspection and memories.

I could never have predicted that I would be on this plane with Archie. In one sense it was a completely fortuitous circumstance, but in another it seemed as though my life was on a trajectory established for me long ago. It seemed as if this trip was taking me somewhere important, a place I needed to be. Although I had no idea what would come of it, the journey seemed portentous, the fulfillment of some vague yearning that occupied the liminal recesses of my mind. I had been working so hard for so long that I had had little time to be reflective. I had been planning to establish a practice in New York City, where I'd done my surgical training as soon as I finished my fellowship with Sir Archibald,, but there was something immensely appealing about Africa which might change my immediate plan. Was Africa not only a place but a symbol? Did it represent that missionary journey that all good Mormons take? My mentor, Archie, and my friend Mike, had deeply-felt attachments. Would I form a similar attachment? Was this trip, in fact, a mission? Would New York be my career and Africa my ministry?

As I ruminated on my life, the plane droned on. The long flight was interrupted by three fuel stops, in Rome, Cairo, and Khartoum, each place more exotic than the last. Rather than enter the hermetically sealed confines of a 747 and emerge a few hours later in a completely new and foreign place, travel in 1956 required fortitude but rewarded the traveler with a sense of having journeyed. Africa is indeed a long way from London, and was at that time a twenty-four-hour flight in the narrow, noisy confines of a "Super Connie" fuselage and left you in no doubt that you had traveled a great distance. The four huge, eighteen-cylinder Wright engines left your ears ringing and your body buzzing even when they were turned off for refueling. The combined effect of noise, vibration, dehydration, fatigue and confinement all contributed to a sense of unreality and suspended time as the minutes and hours ticked by.

Night was falling by the time we reached the African continent at Cairo and, during the night, we flew the long stretch over Egypt and the Sudan and landed in Khartoum at three o'clock in the morning. Even at this hour there was a soft hot wind blowing across the desert. The terminal was a single building and while waiting for the plane to be serviced, we drank tepid, sickeningly sweet tea. I stood outside savoring my first taste of the "real" Africa. My imagination was running in overdrive reflecting on the history of this intriguing place which Gordon had defended against the onslaught of the Mahdi and his hordes of whirling dervishes, terminating in his gallant death. My senses detected the unique smell of the African desert for the first time; a slightly pungent odor suggesting charcoal fires, human and animal waste, and the bouquet of unknown desert plants. We eventually continued our flight, on over western Ethiopia and down into Kenya, the vast, arid, sparsely-populated countryside, cloaked in darkness, passing beneath us. At long last, as dawn was breaking the morning of the day after leaving England, the pilot announced that we were on final approach to Nairobi (Embakasi) International Airport.

Nairobi is located on a high plateau to the west of the Athi Plains, about 100 miles south of the equator, at a height of 5,500 feet above sea level. The altitude moderates the temperature, which seldom rises much above eighty degrees Fahrenheit and the average annual rainfall is only about thirty inches. The climate couldn't be more different from London's, although it isn't entirely dissimilar to my family's ranch in Utah. The Indian Ocean lies about 300 miles to the southeast and Lake Victoria about 160 miles to the northwest. Nairobi National Park, a forty-four-square mile game reserve, is almost contiguous with the city and, as we descended in the morning light, I could see the park but could only imagine the animals that populated it. I knew something of the place from books, but this was my first real look at the legendary city that had been the headquarters of big game hunters and adventurers since the earliest days of British colonization.

After an uneventful landing (the best kind) we disembarked from the plane and were driven to the terminal in buses. Nairobi airport looked like a United Nations waiting area with whites in khakis, Indians in turbans, and Africans in an array of colorful clothes, including the ubiquitous blue jeans. We loaded our luggage into Mike's car and started off towards the small farm that Mike and his wife Sue owned in Limuru, several miles to the northwest of Nairobi. As we sped along the ochre-colored dirt road, I saw Africa for the first time in the daylight. The palette of colors was different from anything I had ever seen: the red earth, trees bursting with purple, orange and crimson flowers and hues of many different colored bougainvillea everywhere.

Women walked along the side of the road, bent almost double, carrying immense loads of wood on their backs, the weight of the load being taken up by a harness around their foreheads. "There you see the work horses of Africa, and yet our future will come to depend on the women." said Mike. The surrounding countryside was verdant with perfectly manicured rows of tea bushes, coffee, and vegetable farms. To protect the people from the Mau Mau rebels, the people were concentrated in *makuti*-thatched huts in villages surrounded by moats protected with a ring of outfacing spiked wooden branches shaved to razor sharp points. Children of all ages and sizes were everywhere. I was disappointed that most were in tattered Western clothes. I guess I expected to see people in skins and loin cloths even this close to Nairobi. I tried to take in all of the sights although in my state of fatigue and excitement it all seemed unreal. Most of the faces I saw were black, although Caucasians and Indians were also much in evidence in 1956.

Mike said that he had arranged a surgical schedule filled with patients at the principal government hospital, the Princess Elizabeth, which became the Kenyatta National Hospital following independence. We would begin early the next morning. Within a day of leaving London, we would be in the surgical suite, hard at work. Much of it would be "routine" plastic surgery, Mike said, but for me it would be my first exposure to some of the surgical problems unique to tropical Africa. I eagerly looked forward to the experience. And after a meal, a stretch and a good night's sleep, I would be ready.

The term "jet lag" didn't enter the English vocabulary until 1969, but the next morning I was jet-lagged nevertheless. Nairobi is only two (or three) time zones east of London, but after the long flight it seemed like much more. I rose and shook the cobwebs from my brain, reminded myself where I was and tried to ignore my out-of-synch circadian rhythm which told me to go back to bed. Doctors are used to sleep deprivation, and fatigue was quickly overcome by excitement. This was going to be an interesting day, full of more pathology than I would see in a lifetime of medical practice in England or America. What Mike described as "routine surgery" wasn't routine at all by Western standards. After breakfast, we drove the short distance to the hospital.

The Princess Elizabeth had an entire ward filled with children with hideous burn deformities. I had never experienced anything like it. It was the first time I had seen the results of burn healing where no skin grafts had been done to cover the wounds. Mike explained that burns, especially of children, are common in Africa where most of the cooking is still done over open fires. Children, especially those with epilepsy, often fell into fires and sustained severe burns which, lacking the proper early care (skin grafting), resulted in massive scar tissue formation. The scar tissue then produced grotesque deformities: hands, arms, and legs bent and fixed into functionless positions; total destruction of the skin of the neck, often with the head literally fused to the chest. Such gross deformities, I learned, are ubiquitous in Africa. The pity is that most could have been avoided by a simple technique of skin grafting, a procedure that can easily be taught to any reasonably skilled doctor.

After visiting the ward, Archie, Mike and I scrubbed and headed into the surgical theater. There, one after another, we treated a succession of children, removing scar tissue and performing skin grafts; straightforward but satisfying work. Then, after lunch, I was brought a patient, a young girl, with an African disease called cancrum oris (*noma*), something I would see much more of in subsequent visits to Africa. It was the first case I had ever seen. Half of her face was missing and her jaws were frozen shut. We spent the early afternoon working to surgically open her jaw joint and replacing the joint surface with a piece of cartilage from one of her ribs so that she could chew food, and reconstructing the hole in her face with grafts of healthy soft tissue from her adjacent cheek. It was a much more challenging procedure than the simple skin grafts and would require several follow-up operations by Mike. Then, in the late afternoon, we operated on three children and one adult with congenital cleft lip (harelip). Older children or adults with unrepaired cleft lip are a rarity in the Western world, but not uncommon in the Third World where repair of such deformities in newborns is rarely done.

By the end of this first day in Africa I felt exhausted but exhilarated. It may seem odd that in the midst of all that suffering and deformity anyone could find joy. For a visiting surgeon, however, the Princess Elizabeth Hospital was a place of deep fulfillment. First of all, we were really helping people, restoring deformed bodies in significant and often dramatic ways. But we were also exercising our craft, our surgical skills, solving complex problems and treating pathologies that most Western surgeons would never encounter in an entire lifetime of work. Plastic surgery is a wonderful discipline in that it depends on knowledge, training and critical skills in combination with hands-on, manual labor. Dexterity of both mind and fingers is required to be a good surgeon. Consequently, at the end of the day I experienced the intellectual satisfaction of having formulated solutions to new problems and the pride of a seamstress whose perfect stitches were tangible proof of her abilities. Few disciplines demand more of both body and mind.

After a very full week of surgery in Nairobi, Archie decided it was time to get out of town and head for Ol Orien, his vast wheat farm on the lower slopes of Mt. Kilimanjaro. The farm was located near the small village of Ol Molog, a Maasai name for "little pimple", describing a hill in the middle of Archie's farm. Mike had just learned to fly in his single-engine Piper Tripacer airplane, and was anxious to show off this new skill to his two somewhat skeptical passengers. When I saw the plane at Wilson Airport, however, I was even more skeptical. The little Piper held four passengers, if they were not too fat, had a four-cylinder air-cooled engine that looked as though it belonged in a Volkswagon and was constructed out of steel tubing covered with fabric. I would come to love this little airplane later on, and even learn to fly one like it, but at first glance it looked mighty tiny and frail.

All apprehension left as soon as we got off the ground. The flight was to last a little over an hour and cover about a hundred miles. From the air I got my first glimpse of rural, real Africa. Mike took off and flew almost due south, towards Kilimanjaro, and as soon as we cleared the city, descended to 100 feet so that Archie and I could get a closer look at the countryside. As we buzzed along at about a hundred miles an hour, the noise of the plane's engine and its shadow skimming along the ground startled the small herds of game that inhabited the plains southest of the city. Zebras scattered in clouds of dust in every direction, kicking their hooves, bucking and snorting. Giraffes, who were less impressed, gazed up at us with their long arching necks; a few sped away with a long, loping grace. Astonished kongoni (hartebeest) charged with their horns low to the ground, searching for the cause of the sudden disturbance.

The plains were dotted with acacias and animal trails criss-crossed the parched earth. Dry river beds wandered randomly across the land. In the midst of this magnificent landscape we passed several Maasai *manyattas*—circles of thornbush that formed corrals filled with round huts made of a frame of sticks plastered with mud and dung. Young Maasai boys tending herds of goats and cattle waved at the plane, spears and herding sticks in hand, their glistening black bodies flashing from under ochre-colored blankets flapping in the wind. It was like living a dream. The freedom of flight, the vast landscape (with Kilimanjaro in the background), the exotic animals, the strange but beautiful Maasai. I thought I would burst from excitement. I caught a glimpse of Archie sitting in the rear seat. The look in his eye said, "I told you so."

Gradually, the great mass of Kilimanjaro became more distinct in the clouds through the windscreen. The snow cap of Kibo, rarely visible in the heat of the day, was covered by a puffy cumulus cloud. The mountain seemed to float, mirage-like, suspended above a layer of glass. Heat waves shimmered from the baked plain beneath. As the ground began to rise toward the mountain, Mike advanced the throttle to full power. The tough little engine changed from a steady purr to a complaining whine as we climbed another 1,000 feet to approach the grass landing strip through a wheat field on the mountain slope. The terrain was changing now as we drew closer to the foothills of the mountain. The parched ground was giving way to an increasingly green landscape. Suddenly a patchwork of golden squares appeared; huge wheat farms, stretching for miles, covered the slopes below.

The engine pitch changed again as Mike eased the throttle back and pulled on the carburetor heat control, preparing to land. Suddenly he banked the plane into a sharp turn and a narrow grass landing strip appeared in the midst of the wheat field before us. Mike leveled the wings, lined up with the center of the strip and landed. We bumped along between the rows of wheat, wing tips gently dusting the ripe golden kernels and came to a gradual halt. We were met on the airstrip by a Land Rover and taken directly to Archie's farmhouse.

We were tired and welcomed the prospect of traditional British afternoon tea before we set to the task of unpacking and settling in. I was about to take my first sip, when the door of the farmhouse sprang open and a handsome weather-beaten woman burst into the room. She looked like farm women everywhere and could easily have been from Montana. "Archie!" the woman exclaimed, "I'm so glad you're here, I need your help with an emergency. There's been an accident on my farm. Please come quickly and have a look."

Archie, unfazed, introduced me to Joan Freyberg, who along with her husband Brian, owned the farm next door. She told us that one of her African farm workers had caught his hand in a rotating gear in a tractor, badly crushing three fingers. She had bandaged the hand as tightly as she dared to control the bleeding, but dared go no further on her own. She was convinced from her brief examination that he needed immediate surgery to salvage as much of his hand as possible.

I had not yet had my experience with the Maasai *moran*, although that would happen soon, and had never before performed surgery in the bush. Archie decided that this was an ideal opportunity for me to treat an emergency under less than ideal conditions. It was serious but not life-threatening and Archie, with a twinkle in his eye and without even rising from his chair, asked me if I could "pop down" to the Freyberg's farm and deal with the situation. The thought of it filled me with apprehension.

I stammered out that we had no instruments, anesthetics, antibiotics or drugs of any kind in our duffles—a situation which seemed of little consequence to Archie. Joan assured me that she did have an instrument kit at her farm that might do. I looked at Archie and Mike, who looked back at me with a combination of pity and amusement. "Get on with it!" Archie said, and I complied.

A moment later I was in Joan's Land Rover, heading down the road toward her farm. We arrived in a flurry of red dust. Joan leaped from the car, ran into the house and returned carrying her instrument kit. The kit contained, to my consternation, an ancient scalpel which obviously had been sharpened many times; a pair of suture scissors, worn but usable, thumb forceps for holding tissue, a few hemostats for clamping bleeding vessels, and a suture needle with a spool of ordinary cotton thread. Despite my more than six years of surgical training, I felt insecure. She informed me that she had no local anesthesia, but we could give him a couple of shots of Scotch. If he is like most Africans around here, she said, his pain threshold is very high.

We headed off towards the machine shop and found the patient waiting. The man was a young adult who sat quietly with a stoic but concerned expression. As I examined his wounded hand he watched me with interest. It was clear that the injury would require amputating at least two of the injured fingers and maybe more. I persuaded Joan to help me move him to the cleaner environs of her home for the surgery. With the patient settled as comfortably as possible, I excused myself to return to Archie's farm on the pretext that I was searching for more instruments. Actually, I needed advice. I jumped into the Land Rover and drove as fast as I could back down the dirt road to Archie.

I can't do this, I told him. I explained that there was no anesthetic, the instruments were pitiful and I was really concerned about sterility. The amputation of at least two, and maybe more of his fingers was going to be necessary. If we could get him to hospital, there was a slim chance that we could save them, but not in a farmhouse with the instruments available. Besides, what in the hell, I wanted to know, am I going to use for anesthesia?

Archie was unmoved. He calmly told me that I was no longer in East Grinstead or New York. He told me I was spoiled. It was true. I was used to working in operating rooms where every technique, instrument and medical gadget was to hand. In Africa, Archie said, I must learn to work with what was available, even if it meant going without anesthetists, skilled surgical nurses or even proper light. It will do you good, he said, to get your feet wet and experience how difficult it is to deal with emergency situations under less than ideal conditions. Often, he reminded me, there is simply no one else available to deal with a problem. Anyway, he concluded, Mike has returned to Nairobi and there is no one else to take care of this man except you and me. And I am turning it over to you, so you had just as well get on with it.

I was slightly wounded by Archie's tone, but it was clear that I had no option but to go ahead. Years later, I understood that he was teaching me an important lesson; that he was preparing me for work under difficult conditions to come. It took a while for me to appreciate it, but in the years that followed I put this lesson to good use many times. Resigned to my task, I drove back to Joan's farm where she and the patient were waiting.

The surgical problem was not particularly complicated. The injury had almost, but not quite, amputated the ring and long fingers, which were hanging by a small bridge of skin, tissue and tendons. The bones were almost cut clean through. The index finger was also injured, but not to the extent of the other two. The injuries were close to the palm and it would be a relatively simple surgical procedure, because the amputations only needed to be completed and the wounds stitched together.

As I stood there, contemplating what to do, Joan explained that Africans, especially rural Africans, are superb patients able to endure much pain without complaining. She believed that many Africans had mastered the art of self-hypnosis, a necessary strategy for dealing with painful and traumatic situations. Such tribulations were a normal part of life and therefore were tolerated without complaint. The closer to basics people are, she speculated, the less they were burdened with the excess emotional baggage carried by most westerners.

Thankful for this encouragement but not really reassured, I told her that I was also concerned about clean water to boil and sterilize the instruments; and what would we do for bandages? Joan assured me that well water was clean and plentiful. She suggested freshly ironed, torn up sheets for bandages. She explained that the bed linen was cleaned by boiling and thus was relatively sterile. Joan was obviously a trooper, well able to make do. She had been through similar situations in the past during her years in Africa.

It took a while to boil the water and sterilize the instruments, and after an hour or so of preparation, I began the surgery. I started by cutting the connecting strands of skin and tendons, tying off the open blood vessels, and carefully sewing skin over the raw ends of the bones and joints. I used the ordinary cotton thread from Joan's kit as suture material. A glass of Scotch was the sole anesthetic, to my intense consternation.

As I worked, I glanced at the man's face from time to time, but aside from a glazing of his eyes, I saw no reaction. He let out a grunt when I cut through bone, but still did not try to withdraw his hand. He did not sweat and his eyelids, aside from an occasional flicker, did not register severe pain. In fact, he watched every move I made with intense concentration. He was certainly not the writhing, sweating, complaining, panic-stricken patient doctors so often see in emergency rooms in the US. It seemed as if I was suffering more for him than he was for himself.

The surgery took about forty minutes, and as I tied off the last stitch I suddenly experienced an enormous sense of relief. I gave Joan instructions on how to care for the wound and then asked her to drive me back to Archie's farm. As we bumped down the road I could feel the tension flowing out of my body. It was late afternoon and the sun was starting its descent to the horizon. As we pulled up to the front porch at Ol Orien I found Archie in a magnanimous mood. He was sitting comfortably in his chair and had obviously switched from tea to a sundowner of Scotch.

Joan waved at Archie as I got out of the car, and then drove off. As I approached the steps Archie motioned for me to sit down and offered me a drink. I didn't need to be asked twice. I told him about the operation in great detail, as I grew progressively more mellow from the Scotch. "You can call yourself a bush surgeon now," Archie said. I nodded in agreement, although I wasn't sure I had earned the title yet.

The next morning my medical training resumed. At Archie's farm, indeed everywhere in Africa when a doctor is present, a daily sick call occurs. African patients are eager for medical care whenever a professional is available. This is in addition to their on-going care from traditional ("witch doctor") healers. Every day that Archie was in residence on his farm a group of patients would gather to see him. He was referred to as the Bwana Daktari, Swahili for doctor. Like patients in the West, Archie explained, Africans always expected medicine (*dawa*) to be dispensed. It was useless, he said, to try to convince them that medication is not always indicated and that they might recover on their own without drugs.

Physicians everywhere, rather than argue the point, often prescribe medicine for patients whether it is truly indicated or not. Just try to convince a Western mother that her baby, who has a viral infection, does not really need an antibiotic which in fact may even do more harm than good. In Asia or India, physicians prescribed herbs or homeopathic medicines. In Africa, a handful of aspirin tablets often sufficed. Mike

Wood, an old hand at this sort of thing, taught me that to really convince a patient of the potency of the *dawa*, the administration of Epsom salts (a strong laxative) was proof that a medicine was indeed powerful and therefore effective.

Archie treated everyone who came to see him with dignity, and the two of us saw several patients each day, often for minor maladies. Over the years he had earned the respect and love of the local people. I learned a great deal watching him and Mike Wood. The farm was an important place for Archie and the people who lived around it were an integral part of its magic. When not seeing patients, we visited with Robin Johnson, who lived on the farm year-round. Robin was his partner and old friend from World War II when Robin had been a fighter pilot for the RAF. The two of them had the unspoken closeness that came from years of mutual respect and love. I accompanied Archie and Robin around the farm on horseback where Robin pointed out its various tracts of wheat, pyrethrum, outbuildings, wells and wildlife and the small villages that had been built to house farm employees. It was a place of amazing beauty, nestled against the foothills of Kilimanjaro on one side and looking out towards the vast expanse of the Nyiri Desert and the Maasai-Amboseli game reserve on the other.

On the last week-end of this, my first visit to Africa, another emergency presented itself. This time it was the Maasai warrior who had been gored by the rhino described in the opening pages of this book. This second emergency was much more serious and the surgery considerably more nerve wracking than the first, and of course I complained about the lack of instruments all over again, but survived it, this time with Archie's help. After Mike flew the Maasai off to the hospital at Arusha, he returned to pick up Archie and me, and we flew back to Nairobi for a few more days of non-stop surgery at the Princess Elizabeth Hospital and at Gertrude's Garden, a hospital for sick children.

The surgical schedule in Nairobi that Mike had arranged for us was all consuming. Day after day we operated from dawn until dark, working on a myriad of patients with cleft palates, harelips, burn wounds, wounds caused by animal bites and maulings, cancer, trauma, and the hideous unique deformities caused by exotic tropical infections such as *noma* and yaws.

Yaws, I learned, was common in East Africa, a disease that in many ways mimicked syphilis. In fact, it too was caused by a microscopic organism called a spirochete. Cancrum oris (*noma*), Mike explained, was caused by a combination of microbes, but not much was known about this destructive disease which was unique to the tropics. Both diseases result in the death of tissue which eventually sloughs away, leaving gaping wounds of the face.

Each patient was a unique challenge, testing all of the ingenuity and skill we could muster. Throughout these challenging days Archie, Mike and I had been operating together as a team, sharing the responsibility and experience. A surgical camaraderie quickly developed from the concerted and intimate effort; the kind of relationship that bonds surgeons treating catastrophes of nature or war. Although I had known Archie and Mike for only a few months, I was already profoundly affected by them. No one had inspired me professionally to that degree before.

On the last weekend of the trip, our surgical schedule for the week complete, Archie, Mike and I returned to Ol Orien. Piling into Mike's little airplane we made the joyous journey to the farm, skimming across the African plain, whooping it up like three giddy children. It was late afternoon, and the acute angle of the sun highlighted the landscape, shading every geological feature. The sky was crystal clear and as we approached Kilimanjaro it was devoid of its usual cloud cover. Rising to almost 20,000 feet in front of us was the glistening snow cap of Kibo, one of the two peaks of the mountain. In the rays of the setting sun, it glowed orange-pink. Below the snowline, the dense rain forest was changing color into hues of blue, green and purple in the fading light of the equatorial sun. The moment was magical.

Before us lay Archie's farm, where thousands of acres of ripe yellow wheat shimmered and rippled in the late afternoon breeze. The colors changed continuously from moment to moment. Beyond the wheat fields the terrain plunged sharply to the great plains below. The distant horizon was sharply defined one moment, and the next became indistinguishable from the sky. The panorama in every direction was breathtaking. I savored this rare moment of beauty, one of the fixed frames in my memory, never to be forgotten. The mystique of Africa cannot be explained or described, it must be experienced. It is easy to believe that mankind originated here in this infinite, enigmatic land. The beauty that surrounded us sealed a shared sense of camaraderie that would bind us together for the rest of our lives.

I felt a strong attraction to Africa even though I had been there but a short time. It was not at all what I had anticipated it to be. My scanty knowledge of Africa derived from reading adventure books and from the movies I had seen. None of these prepared me for the real Africa. Most first-time visitors are instantly attracted to this land, many become intrigued, even consumed, by the mystery and beauty of it. A few are repelled, sometimes frightened as though some dark secrets are hidden there that are best left undisturbed. Perhaps, lurking in our collective consciousness is the knowledge that Africa is the cradle of humankind.

Mike circled the airstrip to make sure that there were no obstructions (such as wild animals grazing), came around and brought us bumpily in. The noise of the airplane had alerted Robin Johnson, who met us with the Land Rover and drove us to the house. In a few minutes we were settled on the veranda for our sundowners. The panorama from the porch was just as spectacular as it was from the air. The majesty of it was overwhelming. We sat there for a moment in silence, taking it all in. Not one of us had an inkling that we were bonding in a relationship that would over the ensuing four decades affect the lives of thousands upon thousands of people. In a reflective mood, Archie broke the silence, speaking what we all had on our minds.

"We must do something about this," he said. "All of these patients with deformities can be treated. We must think of some way to provide help for as many as possible." Those who were providing medical care in Africa at the time were simply overwhelmed by the sheer volume of patients who needed care. It was frustrating not to be able to help all of them. Prior to Mike's return to East Africa as a qualified plastic surgeon, only those very few patients who were treated by Archie on his annual visits benefited from plastic and reconstructive surgery. Archie's comment expressed the frustration felt by all of us. It seemed inconceivable that so many people were forced to go through life deformed, sequestered from society and often their families too, when surgery could improve their lot.

It was easy to be overwhelmed by the sheer size of the problem, to simply give up, and it was tempting to say that there was really nothing one person (or three) could do. I wondered how we could possibly make a dent. The logistics of providing surgical care to so many patients seemed hopelessly complicated. Where could we find support for volunteer surgeons, anesthetists and nurses, provided we could even recruit them? Where could we find the start-up money to launch such a project? We would need to provide living quarters, subsistence, supplies, food and transportation.

Mike reckoned that he could provide continuity, because he lived full time in Africa. Much of the preliminary planning could be done by him. It was obvious that as the only plastic surgeon in this vast area Mike could work twenty-four hours a day for the rest of his life and barely make a difference to the patient load. Even with a constant flow of volunteers to help him, it was clear that we would still fall far short of being able to operate on all of those who needed it, but with sensible planning, there was much that could be accomplished. "It may seem like a drop in the ocean, operating on a few patients," said Mike, "but at least it is better than doing nothing."

I believed that I could recruit American surgeons to work for short periods, perhaps a couple of months or so. Few surgeons would be in a position to leave their practices and come to Africa for long periods. But it would be a unique opportunity for young surgeons in the period after they finished their training but before they established a busy practice. I also thought that such an experience would appeal to older surgeons who were winding down their careers and might want to have an adventure. We agreed that teaching should hold a high priority. It is not difficult to teach any reasonably skilled doctor how to cut and apply a simple skin graft to cover a burn or how to repair a cleft lip. The visiting surgeons would be rewarded by the rich opportunity to see and treat such a varied spectrum of surgical problems, many of which they would never see in a lifetime of practice at home, in America or Europe.

I volunteered to do what I could in the US and Canada. Archie said that he would do the same in England. With Archie's enormous influence in plastic surgery, I had no doubt that he would be successful. In retrospect, it is remarkable how naive we were. We had no idea of the problems we would encounter. Raising money is always difficult. Raising money for projects in remote Africa proved extraordinarily difficult. Our plan of using a rotating list of surgeons was optimistic at best. As time proved, very few surgeons were able to volunteer and participate in Third World medical projects; not nearly as many as we projected. Also, we vastly underestimated the cost of such an undertaking: the costs of transportation, supplies, housing, and so forth. However, our enthusiasm overcame these mundane considerations, and fortunately so, for had we heeded the drawbacks and abandoned our plans in the beginning, the Flying Doctors would never have come into being.

Mike was adamant that we use light airplanes as the principal means of transportation to rural "bush" hospitals. It was not possible to transport the many patients from the rural areas who required plastic surgery treatment to the few urban hospitals in East Africa. The uniqueness of the plan was that the surgeons would travel from one rural hospital to another, performing surgery at each one on a regularly scheduled basis. The patients would be triaged and collected at the hospital when the surgical team arrived. Travel by automobile was too time consuming and impractical. Many of the roads become impassable in the rainy season. The advantage of air travel was obvious. Mike's idea of using airplanes came from the Australian Flying Doctor Service which had been in operation for several years, but differed from our plan because it employed mostly general practitioners to bring basic medical care to remote areas. Transporting surgical specialists was not deemed practical in Australia at that time.

As the light faded and darkness descended, we talked on and on into the night, "brain busting" ways to bring our newborn concept to fruition. Details were hazy but the overall project started to take shape. I went to bed that night with my head spinning with the excitement we had generated. What young man wouldn't? It was heady stuff. Here I was on the side of the highest mountain in Africa with two men I admired, dreaming of doing something exciting in the world; a challenge that promised to add spice and adventure to my life, as well as help people in need. This was more than a vacation. I had found my mission.

3

Anticipation

At the beginning of 1960 the Flying Doctors of East Africa was just three years old and suffering growing pains. A lot had happened in those first three years. We owned two airplanes, including Mike's Tripacer. The second plane, a Piper Aztec, a gift from Arthur Godfrey, had just entered service. And a third plane, also a gift from Arthur Godfrey (and "Pudge" Piper), a Piper Cherokee was on its way. Tragically, our mentor, Sir Archibald McIndoe was to die suddenly of a heart attack in April. It was Archie's extraordinary ability to stimulate and challenge his students that had resulted in our plan to bring plastic surgery to the bush in East Africa. Mike and I were deeply saddened by the news.

Mike Wood and Hillary Prendergast, our first surgical nurse, flew a regular schedule of surgical safaris to mission hospitals in rural Kenya and Tanzania with the occasional help of surgeons visiting from abroad. I had been able to manage only two working trips to Africa during the three years. I was struggling hard to get my own career on the road in New York City after serving a two-year hitch in the United States Navy, and between a teaching appointment at New York University and my evolving practice, I had very little free time. What free time I did have was spent expanding the Flying Doctors organization (officially called AMREF) in America, and in the odious but necessary task of raising money for our African venture. Progress was agonizingly slow, but with the help of Mike and Sue Wood, who made a couple of trips to America, we were making progress.

One day my wife Nan complained that she was fed up with hearing Mike and me constantly talking about Africa and the Flying Doctors. She declared that she was ready to go with me on my next trip and "see what this obsession with Africa is all about." Nan had a legitimate beef. She was a tireless worker in our fundraising efforts. She had watched the development of the Flying Doctors from the first—but from afar, from America. My fervor had rubbed off on her and she had become involved in our dream. Nan is not the type to be involved in anything vicariously, she is an activist, a hard worker for what she believes in. Nan had not yet been to Africa, and was eager to go.

Nan wanted to be useful in a hands-on way. She wanted to be of practical help on surgical safaris. During 1957 and 1958, while I was in the Navy for a second hitch, Nan convinced the operating room supervisor at the Naval Hospital to give her a personalized mini course in basic operating room technique, so that she could set up an operating room, sterilize instruments, lay out the table, assist at surgery, and generally make herself useful when trained help was scarce, as is often the case in the Third World. This condensed training proved most helpful in the bush many times.

I called Mike in Nairobi, announcing Nan's desire to come along with us on our next surgical trip. Mike thought it a wonderful idea and immediately set about making arrangements. I was happy to give the news to Nan at dinner that evening, that we were going on a surgical safari with Mike. "You'll get a real taste of bush surgery and we can take a little extra time and see a bit of East Africa," I promised. I planned a six-week working trip. The pull of Africa was strong, and I was longing to get back in touch with the basic world of medical practice there.

In large urban centers such as New York, it is not difficult to lose touch with what the practice of medicine is all about. In big cities, the focus of medical practice is on medical technology, paperwork and a myriad of other unrewarding details of modern hi-tech medical routine, all of which is time consuming. The constant stress of a big city clientele, dealing with the need for immediate gratification, and a high-speed world where perfection is expected at all times, began to take its toll on me. I needed a break from time to time if only to reorient my goals.

Planning such an exciting trip occupied much of our time for several months before our visit and was great fun for Nan and me. We listed every piece of equipment, instrument, syringe, and suture that we thought we would need. Finally, the long awaited day arrived, and we left for East Africa via London on the BOAC "red-eye" flight and arrived in Nairobi at dawn the next day. Mike and Sue Wood met us as we cleared through customs. Mike was in a high state of expectation about our forthcoming safari, and regaled us with stories of his recent adventures on the way from the airport to his home. He had been in touch by radio with the hospitals we were to visit and had asked them to line up patients who required plastic surgery.

Nan and Sue had met briefly in England and later in America where they worked together raising money for the Flying Doctors. They hit it off immediately. Both women were similar; optimists by nature, exuding warmth, boundless energy, they are positive thinkers possessed with an exuberant sense of humor. They became fast friends and have remained so to this day.

Over many cups of tea, Mike and I discussed the problems we were encountering raising the necessary money to fund our projects. Raising money from American donors was particularly difficult since many Americans considered this part of Africa to be a British responsibility. To many people, plastic surgery in Africa seemed remote and even an elitist enterprise. They did not understand that plastic surgery is not only face-lifting, not just cosmetic surgery, but reparative surgery in the broadest sense of the word. Raising money for a project in Africa was especially difficult.

Mike told me that he and Sue had taken over a farm on the slopes of Kilimanjaro, next door to Archie McIndoe's "Ol Orien", and were working hard to make it productive. Mike was lucky to have such a capable wife as Sue who really managed the farm while Mike spent so much time traveling in the Tripacer to bush hospitals. Fortunately, the farm was producing a basic living for them. Mike's private practice of plastic surgery in Nairobi was not sufficient to meet all expenses—paying patients were few and far between in Nairobi in those days. Plastic surgery was just beginning to take hold in 1960. There was no financial compensation for the work Mike was doing in the mission and government hospitals.

That night, Nan's first in Kenya, the four of us enjoyed dinner together. Mike gave us a rundown on what our surgical safari would entail over the next few days. Mike and I were to operate the next morning at the Princess Elizabeth Hospital (now the Kenyatta Hospital) with Dr. Ralph Bowen, a CARE-MEDICO fellow. The Kenyatta is still the principal teaching hospital in Kenya. Mike, Sue, Nan, and I met later in the day for lunch at the famous Thorn Tree, the sidewalk cafe at the New Stanley Hotel. It has been said that if you sit long enough at one of the tables of the Thorn Tree you will see everyone you know. Certainly you would see everyone you had ever met in East Africa.

Flushed with excitement, Nan explained that Sue had taken her on a tour of the colorful Nairobi market where every conceivable local product was on display for sale. The shops were full of artefacts, paintings, wood sculptures, antiques, tribal paraphernalia, clothing, and the like. Nairobi was one of the most colorful cities on earth. Sparkling with well-tended lawn-lined streets, ablaze with the color of tropical flowers, the city was clean and bright. The mass migration of the rural poor to the city had not yet begun. Beggars and the homeless were not in evidence. An air of bustle and business permeated the city, a legacy from the English tempered by the relaxed mode of the tropical locals. Mugging and personal street crimes were almost unheard of. One could walk safely anywhere in the town, night or day. In fact, if caught, a robber faced the fury of the mob. Only the prompt arrival of the police prevented serious injury and even death to a robber at the hands of the crowd.

Fascinating people crowded the Nairobi streets. Up-country ranchers in khaki shorts and broad-brimmed hats, men in business suits tailored on Saville Row, Somalis in wildly colorful robes (Somali women are amongst the most beautiful on earth), Africans of all cultures and tribes in *kikois* and *kangas*, Indians in turbans and saris, policemen in immaculate starched white and khaki uniforms, explorers, hunters, priests and preachers all added to the scene. Burgeoning numbers of African businessmen and politicians were beginning to appear in restaurants and bars previously reserved for white colonials.

Hunting safaris began at either the New Stanley or the Norfolk Hotels. It was commonplace to see an entire safari with open safari cars, Land Rovers, Bedford trucks and large staffs waiting in front of the hotel to pick up their clients. The white hunters looked like white hunters should; rugged men, young and old, with bush clothes, handlebar moustaches and sunburned skin. The African trackers dressed in starched and knife-sharp pressed khakis. Never a dull moment at the Thorn Tree.

Mike cautioned that we had plenty of time for lunch, but we could not dawdle too long afterward, as we had to get on to Wilson Airport for a three-hour flight to Mombasa on the coast. It was necessary to get there before dark as there were no lights on the landing field and the Tripacer was not the fastest airplane in the world. A car would be waiting to take us to the Kaloleni Mission Hospital. He told us that Kaloleni was the first Christian mission in East Africa, founded on the coast in the mid-eighteen hundreds. He said that the hospital was Anglican and very well run, but poor like so many mission hospitals.

Continuing, we learned that the mission hospitals were dependent on funds raised by their parent institutions in England or the States. If the home church was rich, or able to raise a lot of money for the missions, the field mission was well-equipped and prosperous. If the home church was a poor parish, then the mission suffered. Some of them get by on a very meager allotment. It was often amazing how well they could do on so little. Mike had radioed Kaloleni and told them that I was particularly interested in cleft-lip, palate and facial deformities. He assured me that they would have quite an interesting surgical list ready for us.

Our plan, after Kaloleni, was to fly to Shirati, a Mennonite mission near Lake Victoria in Tanzania, and from there to Kaimosi, an Anglican Hospital near Kisumu in western Kenya. He saved a special surprise for Nan. Sue would join us at the end of our safari at their new farm near Ol Molog on Kilimanjaro. Mike had scheduled four days off to take us on our own private safari to the Ngorongoro Crater and the Serengeti Plains. The wildebeest migration would be in full swing then. Off we would go with just ourselves, a truck and a Land Rover.

Nan was by now ecstatic. The plan exceeded her wildest dreams. A private safari was out of our financial reach, but to go with the Woods would be perfect. Our lunch was delicious and made all the more interesting as we watched the colorful parade of people that passed in front of us. Tourists and Kenyans occupied the tables on the sidewalk of the Thorn Tree. Most were white, and bore the unmistakable stamp of the English who had colonized Kenya; rugged, sunburned, self-sufficient types. A few tables were occupied by black Africans tasting their newborn sense of imminent freedom from British rule. In a few short years the scene would change and the tables would be dominated by Africans and Indians.

Pointing out how the people at lunch seemed to be enjoying themselves, Sue guessed that most of them did not yet fully comprehend the impact independence would have on their lives. Many of the whites, worried about the consequences of a black government in Kenya, had already returned to England. Those that stayed were hoping to continue the status quo of their lifestyle under Jomo Kenyatta's new government. Sue knew that change was inevitable, and with her characteristic optimism about Africa, she believed that there would be room for everyone in the new way of life. She told us that many of the whites were the second and third generation living in Kenya, and considered themselves to be Africans, even though their forebears had confiscated the land very much like the settlers did in America from the American Indians. Sue knew that the black Africans sitting at the tables of the Thorn Tree were about to dominate the country and reckoned that it was high time that they did. She reminded us that many were educated in Europe and had waited a long time to determine the destiny of their country.

During much of our lunch we talked about changes in the medical system that might be expected. Mike reckoned that vast changes were almost a surety. He believed that the country was not prepared for sudden change and hoped that the changes would be gradual. With every politician making demands on the budget, a principal fear was that medical care would suffer unless it had strong advocates. The budget for medical care in new developing countries frequently gave way to other needs, such as agriculture, education, and defense. Colonial rule, for all of its drawbacks, was unique in providing a high level of medical care with dedicated doctors and professionals. What could be expected when that service was handed over to the new government, and what role would the missionary hospitals play?

Having finished lunch and completed our philosophical musings, we headed for Wilson Airport to begin Nan's first surgical safari.

4

The Oldest Mission

As we drove out on the tarmac at Wilson Airport, the little Tripacer was being fueled with avgas at one of the pumps. The Land Rover was full of our personal bags and instrument cases, which we proceeded to load onto the plane. Weight and balance were critical to safe flight, particularly in such a small aircraft, and Mike carefully arranged our baggage in the back of the plane, balancing the load. He then calculated the weight of the fuel, factored in the temperature and the altitude and estimated the speed at which the nearly overburdened Piper would become airborne. Just then a thin, sallow-looking man with thick Coke bottle glasses, sandy red hair and a freckled face walked up to the plane carrying a small bag. He identified himself as a missionary who was on his way back to Kaloleni after home leave. He heard we were flying to the coast and asked if he could bum a ride.

I didn't know a great deal about flying then, it was before I learned to fly myself, but I knew enough to worry about this extra load and whether it would compromise our ability to take off in the hot, thin air of mile-high Nairobi. I thought we already had a very full load with all of our personal baggage, instrument packs, and the three of us. Typical of his good nature in such matters, Mike told our new arrival to hop in the back seat with Nan. At least he was skinny. Mike filed our flight plan with East Africa Control and then taxied out to the end of the runway. Fortunately we were taking off from a long, paved airstrip. After a ground roll that seemed interminably long, the plucky little airplane rose slowly from the ground and ascended into the afternoon sky.

The flight to Mombasa was turbulent in the clear, hot air. Thermals rose from the earth beneath us, heated by the hot tropical sun. As we flew southeast, the flat expanse of the Yatta Plateau was on our left, and the heights of Kilimanjaro, the Chyulu and Taita Hills rose to our right. We flew low over Machakos with its terraced countryside, tended by the Wakamba tribe. From the air it looked like Switzerland, perfectly manicured and green. To Nan's great delight Mike buzzed the elephant herds in Tsavo Park (strictly illegal of course). The distraught females raised their trunks in the air and trumpeted defiantly at this intrusion into their space as they stampeded their young ahead of the plane. "I didn't know elephants were red," exclaimed Nan. She had never seen elephants in the wild before. Mike, somewhat amused, told her that they weren't red, but covered in mud that had dried to red dust.

After a bumpy but beautiful three hours we could see the Indian Ocean in the distance, and a few minutes later we landed on the airstrip at Mombasa. The equatorial sun was rapidly descending below the horizon. An old rickety Land Rover was waiting to carry us on the two-hour trip south to Kaloleni Mission. Soon after we started along the rutted dirt road, the moonless night descended like a curtain. Only the two feeble headlights of the Land Rover illuminated our passage, the light bouncing up and down like a juggler as we navigated the endless ruts and potholes. The equatorial night was inky black. No lights showed along the roadside, only the stars twinkling brightly through the unpolluted sky.

During the entire flight to the coast, the young missionary had spoken very little, and then only when asked a question. He had been engrossed in a paperback book and showed little interest in God's magnificent creation below us. Nan tried once or twice to engage him in conversation, but it was clear that he was either shy or withdrawn, so she left him to his reading. She later said that he seemed exceedingly odd. Once we got in the Land Rover, however, the young man became more talkative during the bumpy night ride, dwelling at length on the sexual mores of the people. He considered the bare-breasted women of the coast clearly lewd and felt personally affronted by the thriving practice of polygamy despite vigorous teachings against it. He explained that he had been on an annual one-month leave from the mission at Kaloleni. He was a bachelor and enjoyed his work at the mission where he was a school teacher for young children, but he was pessimistic, almost cynical, about the prospects for Christian proselytizing of tribal Africans on the coast. He was peculiarly critical of the High Anglican Church, despite his own faith.

The church was too uncompromising, too stuffy, he thought. Africans needed a practical religion, one without ceremonies they didn't understand—as much as they loved pageantry. The formal churches, he told Nan, must learn to approach the people on their own terms. The Catholics were better at it, he thought, because they could adapt to the indigenous culture wherever they were, whether in Africa, Mexico, or South America. The Catholics were willing to play a waiting game; they had time, even centuries, to win the people. In the meantime, they adapted to local needs. We Anglicans, he said, insist on immediate compliance, and it doesn't work that way. As he talked, Nan nodded in response, but said little.

In 1960 he was only expressing what many churches later were forced to recognize, not only in their efforts to win over the developing world, but also in the so-called Western world, too. Contemporary churches which did not topically address the needs of the people experienced hard times when converts demanded a say in doctrinal matters. Blind faith no longer sufficed. He told us that Kaloleni Mission was indeed the oldest on the East African coast. Its constituency was comprised of indigenous tribesman who eked out a subsistence from small farm plots of maize, yams, bananas, coconuts and some domestic animals. They were not fishermen.

I asked the skinny young missionary what percentage of the local people had been converted to Christianity since the inception of the mission. He did not know for sure, but doubted that it was more than fifteen percent of the population, even though a much higher percentage would profess to being Christians. Like many Africans, he said that people clung to old traditional beliefs, preferring to mix their new Christianity with these old beliefs, but embracing tribal tradition if it came to making a choice. He noted that fortunately such a decision was not demanded, at least overtly, by the Church. He felt that the Church realized that it was sometimes best to let sleeping dogs lie.

During my travels in Africa, I gained a healthy respect for the work of missionaries. They were largely unsung heroes who contributed enormously to the well-being of rural Africans, especially in health care and to their progress in education. I found the great majority of them to be hardworking, selfless and dedicated and in almost all cases they sincerely cared about people and not the accoutrements of modern society. Today they are often vilified, unjustly I believe, as being "politically incorrect" in modern Africa.

The young man was uncommonly fixated on the subject of sex; he was a repressed and angry young man and we were relieved to see the lights of the mission off in the distance. We'd had enough preaching for one night.

We arrived at the hospital about nine. The grounds were dark. A generator chugged away in the background, lighting a few dim bulbs in the hospital and the main residence, where we were treated to a cold supper by a taciturn and silent woman. There was only one bath and shower in the compound, we were told. Since Nan was the only female in our party she was assigned the tub first, and shown the way. I followed to see where it was, and then went back to join Mike.

When it seemed as though she was taking an inordinate amount of time, I went to check on her. The tub was outdoors, located on the edge of a terrace looking out into the pitch black expanse of the African night. I found Nan wrapped in towels, hovering on the edge of the tub. She had filled it with hot water, always a precious commodity in Africa, but had not got in. She wasn't herself; she seemed troubled, and looked quite anxious. In the distance I could now hear the beat of tribal drums. The darkness, mystery, and now the drums had unnerved her.

"Darling, you look like you've seen a ghost. What on earth's the matter?" I said. "I feel so stupid. I'm a grown woman and not a child, but as I was getting ready to get into the tub in this dark place, with the drums beating—and that spooky young man that came with us and all—I couldn't help thinking of Janet Leigh in the shower scene in *Psycho*. How utterly stupid and embarrassing, but I couldn't help it. I got scared." I sat with her as she finally took her bath in the lukewarm water. When she was done, I took a cold shower and we walked back to the main house, where we were promptly guided back outside again toward a small round, thatched hut. This hut would be our home for the duration of our stay. It was still pitch black as we made our way along the path, led by one of the staff carrying a kerosene hurricane light. Nan watched every footstep as she searched for snakes and bugs. The drums were still beating in the distance. I could understand her anxiety, her concern. A New York City girl in darkest Africa. Her imagination was running wild.

We awoke early the following morning to a hot cup of tea brought to our hut by a charming young African woman. From outside we heard a loud voice saying, "One-two-three, one-two-three, and now follow me and watch what I do, one-to-three." We looked out the door and to our amazement saw a group of school children of all ages, rows of young black faces in regimented lines and starched uniforms, doing calisthenics under the direction of a young white man. The mysteries of the previous night were gone, only to be replaced by the incongruous scene before us, and the sounds of doves, the chirping of songbirds and the English-inflected cadence count of the drill instructor.

After breakfast of papaya, bananas, and home-made biscuits, we made the short walk to the clinic and had our first real look at the hospital. A long line of African patients were waiting to be examined. The hospital was typical of many rural hospitals in Africa. It was a large square building raised off the ground on short pilings, to avoid flooding during the rainy season. The roof was thatched; an effective method of protecting the inside from rain and the scorching sun, but also serving as an excellent incubator for all manner of vermin; bats, snakes, bugs and the like, all living in symbiosis with their human partners. Such thatching had to be replaced every few years, we were told, at which times the whole village turned out to help. In my mind's eye I could see them removing the roof while a host of small animals fled for cover.

The interior rooms all opened to the outside. The various wards were clean and contained simple cots arranged side by side. Despite the prevalence of malaria, there were no mosquitoe nets or window curtains. Though the value of mosquito nets in the prevention of malaria was understood at that time, they simply were not provided for in most bush hospitals.

The utility rooms, clinic and operating rooms opened to the veranda, which completely encircled the building. On the grounds surrounding the veranda, the patients' families had set up numerous cooking fires and mothers were busily cooking *posho* (ground maize meal) for patients reclining on the cots inside. The warm tropical climate made it possible to conduct the clinics, pharmacy, and dispensary in the open year around. The facilities were simple and sparse, but clean, in spite of the openness and lack of convenience. The nurses and assistants, who were busily attending to their duties, were spotlessly dressed and hygienic. All the staff seemed proud with good morale.

The simple operating theater was typical of many bush hospitals both in 1960 and now. The entry door and windows were open to the warm tropical air. For that matter, there were no window panes to close, but sometimes the openings were covered with gauze sheeting. The simple operating table was an uncomplicated affair with manual controls. The operating lights were fashioned out of cardboard lined with aluminum foil. Electricity was provided by the hospital's diesel generator, and was stored in a series of old 12-volt batteries. Daylight or a kerosene lamp was sometimes the primary source. In night emergencies, when all else failed, power was provided by a Land Rover or truck parked outside with its engine running, jumper cables connected to the operating theater's 12-volt lights.

The chief physician was a man named Evans. He explained that *pombe* (palm wine) filled many hospital beds in Kaloleni. Since the wine is fermented high in the coconut trees, some of the intoxicated "workers" would fall out of the palms and often break several bones, requiring weeks of hospitalization and loss of work. I'd heard of people injured from falling off a bar stool, but never out of a palm tree. After fermentation, the alcoholic content of this native drink was very potent, probably around 150 proof. Many beds were tied up by these orthopedic problems—beds that could have been well utilized otherwise. Alcoholism had its price in Africa too.

Gynecologic problems were common also, Dr. Evans said, occupying many additional beds. Huge benign tumors of the uterus (fibroids) were frequent. He told us that for centuries newborns with congenital deformities had been abandoned in the bush to die from exposure or be devoured by hyenas, jackals and vultures. The church had made great efforts to change this custom, but had only partly succeeded. Such a tradition possibly accounted for the significantly lower incidence of cleft-lip in Africans. It was a brutal form of social Darwinism but its effects were measurable. In fact, harelip or cleft palate is only one-fifth as common in people of African descent. I was assured, however, that despite this ongoing custom there were still plenty of cleft problems to care for.

As we were making our tour of the hospital and clinic, Nan saw a crude wooden rack in the utility room next to the operating theater, draped with several pink surgical-gauze sponges. "Why are those sponges pink?" she asked. Dr. Evans explained that they were used over and over, and because is was impossible to wash all of the blood out of them, they were pink. He couldn't afford to use brand new gauze sponges for each procedure, even if we could get them, he added. Nan never forgot that demonstration of frugality. Of course there was nothing wrong with such a process from a medical point of view. The sponges were washed and sterilized and the presence of a pink stain from the breakdown of hemoglobin in the red blood cells was of no medical consequence.

Nan also discovered that soap was a precious commodity. Each and every bar of soap was used until the last bubble had been extracted. We guiltily reflected on the many hundreds of small bars of soap supplied by hotels and motels that are wasted in the Western world. Since that day at Kaloleni, Nan has never left behind a small bar of soap in a hotel. They are collected and transported to Africa on our next visit where our minor thievery is much appreciated by nurses everywhere.

Mike and I examined the patients who had been lined up for us, with Nan taking notes. It was obvious that we couldn't operate on all of them in the three days we had allotted. We had to make a selection and hope that the others could be treated on a subsequent visit. Such choices required tough, sometimes heartbreaking decisions. Which patients had the most urgent need? Which ones could wait? It was always difficult to leave behind patients that you can't help; sometimes it was tragic. I always left a bush hospital with a nagging sense of guilt because I simply couldn't do everything that needed to be done; no one could. Sometimes I tried to harden myself to the choices but it was never easy and I was never really successful.

When our list was complete, Dr. Evans checked to make sure none of our patients had eaten that morning—a necessary precaution to avoid vomiting during anesthesia. Vomiting can result in death from asphyxia, or pneumonia if the patient survives. It was a constant problem in bush hospitals. Mothers could not bear to see their children hungry and often tried to sneak food to them while they awaited surgery. It was impossible to convince all mothers that a hungry child shouldn't be fed before surgery. The logic of withholding food from a hungry baby simply escaped them. The staff had to be constantly alert to this danger. On another trip to a hospital in the north of Kenya, I saw Mike break down in tears when a young boy vomited during ether anesthesia, aspirating the contents of his full stomach into his lungs. He died because his mother had secretly given him a meal of *posho* before surgery, against strict instructions.

The cleft lip surgeries were performed under local anesthesia with sedation provided by a little Scotch in a solution of sugar water. General anesthesia was required for cleft palates and luckily an excellent nurse anesthetist was available at Kaloleni. It would be several more years before the Flying Doctors had the luxury of a full-time anesthesiologist. Consequently, we preferred local anesthesia whenever possible because of its safety.

One patient had elephantiasis, an enormous swelling of the leg and thigh caused by blockage of the lymphatics by filaria, a small worm whose eggs are carried by mosquitoes, a disease not uncommon on the coast. The treatment of such a condition is relatively gross. The leg is suspended in the air by a pulley to facilitate access to its entire circumference. A long incision is made from groin to ankle, going down to, but not including, muscle, and the leg is virtually filleted. All of the skin and fat of the leg is removed as one large block of tissue which is placed flat on a table, and using a skin graft knife, the skin is removed for grafting. After all bleeders have been tied off on the leg, the skin graft is placed over the raw surface of the entire leg and sewn into place. A pressure bandage is wrapped around the leg and changed frequently. This is maintained for several weeks to apply compression to prevent accumulation of blood or edema fluid.

As previously noted, gynecologic problems always occupied many beds. Two female patients had vesico-vaginal fistulas, and one sixteen-year-old had severe scarring of the entrance of the vagina (introitus), the result of female genital mutilation (circumcision) at the age of thirteen in a traditional tribal ceremony. The operation to repair vesico-vaginal fistula is complicated. The vagina was split open along the roof of the canal, isolating the urethral opening from the bladder. To prevent recurrence of the problem, a layer of tissue was placed between the vaginal lining and the bladder restoring the urethra to its normal position. Muscle flaps were used from the inner thigh in the two patients we operated on at Kaloleni.

The after care is as important as the operation in vesico-vaginal fistula repair. A catheter placed in the bladder through the reconstructed urethra must be kept open to divert the urine from the freshly repaired tissues, otherwise the wound would break down and the fistula restored as before. Constant nursing care is required to keep the catheter open and functioning while healing occurs. At Kaloleni, the nursing care was excellent. The African nurses were fastidious about following instructions. We heard later that both patients healed well without recurrence of the fistula.

Despite being outlawed by governments and pressure from many sources, female circumcision is still common amongst many tribes. The practice is rooted in ancient traditions. It is believed that excision of the clitoris, and often the labia too, eliminates sexual pleasure during intercourse for the female, so that she will not be tempted to stray from her husband's bed. The operation is crude, often performed with dull and un-sterile instruments, so that infection is common. Infection and open wounds result in excessive scar tissue which partially or completely blocks the entrance to the vagina, making intercourse difficult, painful and often impossible. Likewise, giving birth presents a *formidable* problem even if intercourse and impregnation are possible. Recurrent bladder infections can occur from blockage of the urethral opening.

This brutal and primitive practice is not altogether opposed by young tribal women who know that without circumcision they have little or no chance of attracting a husband. I recently was told the story of an educated African woman who was employed by the UN in New York, who before returning to her home in a West African country, requested that her twelve-year-old daughter be surgically circumcised by a surgeon in New York. Aghast at the idea, the surgeon asked her why, as an educated woman of the world, she would subject her daughter to such barbarism. She replied that much as she loathed the tradition, her daughter would not be marriageable without the operation, and that she would prefer that it be done under modern sterile conditions in New York rather than by a traditional or untrained operator at home.

Surgical correction of such scarring is difficult but becomes necessary in severe cases, especially if there is obstruction of the urinary or menstrual outflow. Our young patient at Kaloleni had obstruction of approximately two-thirds of her vaginal orifice from scar tissue, the result of excision of her clitoris and a large portion of both labia. Miraculously, she had married, but intercourse proved impossible and giving birth through the birth canal was deemed impossible so that surgical correction was mandatory. The operation consisted of removing the scar tissue which left a large gaping raw area around the entrance of the vagina, which we lined with two skin flaps, one from each inner thigh, which were rotated into the vaginal wound. The open wounds on the inner thighs that resulted from rotation of the skin flaps were covered with free skin grafts, a technique that I employed subsequently on two other patients during my travels in Africa. Several months later, I learned from Michael Wood that the operation had been a success. Hopefully, this ghastly practice of mutilating the genitalia of women will one day be abolished. Although some progress has been made, several cultures are firmly against change.

Most rural hospitals in Africa are faced with treating burns in children. Kaloleni was no exception, Three of the burn patients were children who urgently needed skin grafting. The open burns were seeping vital body fluids, preventing healing and contributing to a general debilitation and anemia. Fortunately blood was available to transfuse those patients. We operated on the burned patients first. We repaired terrible burn scars that fixed elbow joints in flexion, and one patient with her neck fused to her chest. These burn patients provided the opportunity to acquaint Dr. Evans with the technique of skin grafting, a skill he would use the rest of his life. Skin grafting knives are simple and inexpensive. Early on in the surgical safaris, Mike and I decided to supply skin graft knives to surgeons who showed an interest in grafting burns.

We operated on one patient after another well into the night. All went smoothly. Nan was baptized into bush surgery. I was proud of how useful she was with such limited training and experience. The nurses and operating room staff were warm, hospitable, and in all ways helpful to her. The following day was spent much like the first with a long list of surgical cases. Early on the third morning we said good-bye and made the long return drive to Mombasa to continue our journey.

5

A Shriek in the Night

The flight from Mombasa via Nairobi to Shirati mission hospital took most of the morning. Our course took us directly over the great Serengeti Plain, the largest animal reserve in the world. The great game migration, to and fro across the Serengeti beneath us was one of the most spectacular sights in the world. Hundreds of thousands of wildebeests and zebras were on the move, the wildebeests, stopping briefly along the way to birth their calves almost as they traveled, and moving on quickly to avoid becoming a meal for the many carnivores—lions, leopards, cheetahs, and hyenas—that feasted on the herds. The buffalo herds on the Great Plains in America must have looked like this before they were hunted into near extinction. We saw large herds of African Cape buffalo and several families of elephants. Again, to give us a thrill, Mike flew as low as possible for a close-up view.

Shirati is on the southern shore of Lake Victoria, the second largest lake in the world. The buildings of the hospital complex came into view as Mike banked the little Tripacer for a clearing run over the compound.

Shirati, a showplace hospital, was administered by Mennonites from Pennsylvania. Mike told us that it was a first class place, as clean and orderly as any rural hospital in the world. There was a large leper colony of over three hundred patients associated with the hospital, making the place downright biblical, and the Mennonites were experimenting with some innovative rehabilitation techniques for people cured of the active disease to make them self-reliant. It was a showcase among mission hospitals.

The Mennonites were the "liberal" wing of a religious movement dating back to the sixteenth century Swiss Anabaptists, but unlike their conservative brethren, the

Amish, they were actively involved in social aid and relief programs all over the world. Mike admired them because they really lived an ethic of love and self-sacrifice. The Mennonites had been involved in international aid since 1725, in an unbroken and continuous history of selfless service. They were also highly independent, appointing their own ministers and making their own decisions, linked to other Mennonite missions and congregations only through loosely organized "conferences."

According to Mike, they were great missionaries. They clung to their own customs, but in nonjudgmental ways that worked well with the indigenous population. Like the Amish, the women wore long dresses or skirts with bonnets and were dedicated practitioners of the domestic arts. Somehow they managed to avoid the kind of ethnocentric and snobbish judgmentalism that had characterized the skinny Anglican, without compromising their own distinctive and deeply held conviction. Mike was really looking forward to this visit, not least because the Mennonites served up some of the best food in East Africa. The place was run by a Dr. Lester Eshleman, a man Mike thought was as good as they came. Eshleman, among other things, was an avid hunter and always kept his pantry stocked with wild game meat.

The Mennonites at Shirati had built a primitive airstrip as an extension of a soccer field about a mile from the hospital compound. We swooped down over the hospital, to announce our arrival, and then lined up for our approach. On final we could see the strip was lined with people, mostly children of all ages, leaving only a narrow corridor for us to land. It is one of the big problems of bush flying, Mike informed us. The people had no concept of how dangerous an airplane was. They frequently crowded airstrips like this. It made for a very hairy approach and landing. The hazard persists until the propeller stops. Mike always buzzed the strip before landing, but it never seemed to scare anyone away. We landed and bumped down the rough dirt and were immediately surrounded by children who seemed oblivious to the propeller. As soon as we slid out of the plane we were engulfed by a sea of smiling faces and had to push our way through the throng.

Dr. Eshleman, who had come out to meet us, stood a few yards away by the ubiquitous Land Rover. He was tall and lean, a striking figure in his surgical scrubs. He welcomed us warmly and helped us load our baggage in to the car. After a short drive to the hospital compound, we alighted from the Land Rover and were introduced to Dr. Eshleman's wife and the hospital staff who showed us to our room.

According to custom, a standard letter form had been sent to Shirati by our administrator Bill Bunford.

AFRICAN MEDICAL AND RESEARCH FOUNDATION
On Feb. 6, 1960 Drs. Michael Wood and Thomas Rees will visit your Hospital

We would be grateful if you could confirm these dates and let us have an operation list at least a week before the projected visit with these details:

(I) Amount of low cloud, if any.
(II) Thunderstorms in the vicinity or any rain.
(III) Visibility: Smoke haze from bush fires, etc.

Please check the airstrip as follows:-
(1) Length of grass. If it is long or tufted, please cut it and remove hard tufts.
(2) Inspect for and remove ant hills. Fill in any holes.
(3) Mark all trees and sisal poles, particularly on the approaches.
(4) Windsock. If none available, light a small fire.
(5) If your strip is murram or earth with little or no grass cover, overnight or recent rain will cause difficulty in bringing the aircraft to a stop. Drive your Land Rover or car up the whole length of the strip and apply the brakes fully; if the wheels lock and the vehicle skids or leaves deep tracks, the strip is probably unserviceable.
(6) If for any reason the airstrip is unserviceable, place white crosses in the middle and at either end—cloth or pieces of wood, iron, etc., will do so long as they can easily be seen.
(7) Keep all cattle and local inhabitants completely away from the strip when the aircraft is due to arrive. It is most important that all school children should be kept well back from the path of the aircraft: if a tyre should burst, the aircraft might go out of control and run into spectators causing loss of life and/or serious injury.

Short hair and safari clothes soon put Nan in trouble. She traveled in long khaki pants, shirt and bush jacket (all à la Abercrombie and Fitch), and wore her hair short. Previously while driving to the village at West Kilimanjaro, she had tended the Land Rover, while I bought some supplies at an Indian *duka* (shop). I returned to the car to find Nan surrounded by Maasai women who were intent on finding out by the most direct means whether or not this strange human with short hair, dressed in long pants and a shirt, was indeed a woman. One woman had summoned up the courage to feel for Nan's breasts through her shirt. Convinced, the Maasai left a somewhat shaken Nan. This was not to be the last time that Nan's sexual identity was questioned by African women.

At Shirati her clothes once again came under question, only this time by the Mennonite women who were hospitable and welcoming, but seemed uneasy. Clearly something was making them nervous. Eventually Dr. Eshleman's wife summoned up enough courage to explain to Nan that it was customary for Mennonite women to be fully covered with long dresses and bonnets. Apologizing for sounding prudish, she tactfully suggested that Nan wear a skirt to avoid embarrassment to the women who lived and worked at Shirati. She explained that the Mennonite religion believed in modesty and thought it important to teach the Africans modesty by setting an example, and offered to loan a dress to Nan if she did not have one in her duffel. Nan, somewhat embarrassed, apologized for seeming disrespectful. She explained that she was unaware of the problem she might cause. Of course she had a dress (one dress) in her kit and would wear it from then on at Shirati.

That night, after first making rounds at the hospital, as Michael had predicted, we enjoyed an excellent dinner of wild eland roast, pan-browned potatoes and gravy, an assortment of fresh garden vegetables (grown at the hospital), and an exquisite apple pie. It couldn't have been better if we had been at a Mennonite dinner table on a farm in Pennsylvania.

We were weary from traveling all day and the prospect of a bed with soft white sheets awaited us. We excused ourselves after the table was cleared and went to our bedroom, which adjoined the main living area, a large central room in Dr. Eshleman's house. Like everything else in the compound, our room was spotlessly clean and cool, crisp sheets invited us to settle into bed. We yearned for a good night's sleep and this was the most comfortable room we'd had in days. But it was not to be. As we dozed off, we were suddenly awakened by an electrifying, inhuman sound. It was a demented inhuman shriek, unlike anything I had ever heard. We leapt from our bed, pulled on our clothes and ran out into the living room, where we found Dr. Eshleman already standing near the front door. He beckoned us to follow him.

Outside, we found a shadowy figure wrapped in a cloth *kikoi*. It was a woman, shrieking at the top of her lungs; the sound gave me goose bumps. In her arms, was a small newborn child, still glistening from the birth canal. Dr. Eshleman gently removed the baby from its mother's arms and examined it. The baby was dead, undoubtedly stillborn. The wailing continued with other women joining in the din. Suddenly, to our surprise, Dr. Eshleman slapped the woman sharply and issued a stern command in Swahili, which put an end to her cries. Tenderly, he then put his arm around her, speaking in a low comforting tone.

When we went back inside, Eshleman explained that the incredible wail was a traditional response to a baby's death in this part of Africa. If he had not put a stop to it, he explained, the cry would have been taken up by every woman within earshot. It could go on for hours or days, he said, with everyone working up a "right proper hysteria." We spoke to him for a while longer, and then returned to bed. But sleep for that night was finished; we talked about the experience until dawn. The incident was both unnerving and incredibly sad. The woman's wail seemed to come from some unfathomably deep place. Life might be cheap in the bush, but that woman still mourned the death of her baby with the same intensity that one would expect from anyone, anywhere in the world.

Infant mortality in rural Africa is high, fifty percent before the age of five in some areas. At times the survival improves somewhat, only to worsen with a new epidemic of measles, cholera, meningitis, a drought or with a particularly large crop of malaria-carrying anopheles mosquitoes during the rainy season.

Many children die of ordinary infectious diseases such as measles—diseases virtually wiped out by immunization in most of the industrialized world. The worldwide malaria eradication program, sponsored by the World Health Organization in the 1970s, well-nigh eliminated the disease in much of the world, but only temporarily. In recent years malaria has returned with a vengeance. The parasite is resistant to many of the anti-malarial drugs in Sub-Saharan Africa, the Indian subcontinent and Southeast Asia. So-called malignant malaria (falciparum), the most dangerous strain, kills tens of thousands of people each year and the number is increasing. It is calculated that over a million people die from malaria each year in the world, most of these in Africa, and that number is currently increasing at an alarming rate. North America is not immune to this malaria epidemic. The disease recently reappeared in the Southern States of the US, causing much concern among health authorities.

Like most bush hospitals, infant diarrhea constituted a major problem at Shirati. Ignorance on the part of the mothers as to treatment and prevention of this killer disease again contributed to the difficulty of controlling it. The communication problem reminded Nan of an episode she experienced while visiting Sue Wood at their farm on

Kilimanjaro. Wasting, dehydrated and wrinkled, a young baby, dying of diarrhea and malnutrition, was trying but failing to suckle milk from the dried-up breasts of her mother. Feeding the baby a water-salt-sugar formula by mouth, Sue Wood managed to control the diarrhea and restore the baby's electrolyte balance. With patience and repetition, Sue showed the mother how to prepare a nutritious milk-based formula for bottle feeding. Confident that the mother understood the basics of bottle feeding, the baby was left to the care of its mother. Several days later, the mother returned with a dead baby in her arms, apparently the victim of malnutrition. The mother had abandoned the bottle and returned to breast feeding. When asked why she had given up the bottle, she responded by tapping the bottle with her fingers. Hard glass is not a substitute for a soft breast.

The next day found us hard at work again, somewhat sleep deprived, dealing with a long surgical schedule. I had several harelips to repair and Mike was operating on other patients, including leprosy victims, in another room. In this part of Tanzania very large tumors of the lymph glands of children were common. The cause was a virus found in a narrow geographic belt across equatorial Africa. The tumors were known as Burkitt's disease, named after Dr. T. K. Burkitt who studied the problem and identified the virus after many hard years of research at Makere Medical School in Uganda. Mike and I teamed up in an attempt to remove a huge Burkitt's tumor on the neck of a young African boy of about twelve. It was a long, difficult and bloody operation requiring three units of blood which fortunately was available from staff members after cross-matching and typing. While we were successful in removing several large masses in his neck, we were unsuccessful in curing him. He died shortly after surgery. It was probably poor judgement on our part to even attempt it. Extremely complicated operations should be relegated to hospitals with more sophisticated equipment and trained staff. Nevertheless, it was a heart-wrenching experience and another hard-learned lesson. Heroic surgery should be undertaken only when there is no other alternative to saving a life. It is difficult for a surgeon to resist the temptation to accept all comers as surgical candidates. In life-threatening situations, risks must be taken that would otherwise not be acceptable, but the odds must be somewhat favorable.

It was at Shirati that I first learned that gestures of gratitude are a culturally constructed response. Just as pain or love is not always expressed openly, gratitude may not be forthcoming either. Sometimes I thought that I had done a first-class job under difficult circumstances and that my efforts were worthy of appreciation. The repair of an open harelip in New York or London almost always evoked a thankful response from the family. Not necessarily so at Shirati. I proudly returned the babies that I had repaired to the arms of waiting mothers only to observe faces with little or no change of expression. At first I was disappointed and a bit chagrined, until one of the missionaries told me that a demonstration of thanks was simply not in the cultural vocabulary of the local people. They were unquestionably grateful but by tradition they did not express or show it openly.

There were other lessons to be learned, too. I operated on a particularly wide and deforming cleft lip in the infant son of a primitive Bantu woman. I proudly returned the child to her arms after achieving what I thought to be an almost "normal" looking result. I anticipated that she would be pleased, even amazed at this surgical triumph. Instead, she refused to accept the child. To her eyes, the child wasn't hers. She could not account for the difference in the baby's appearance. It took considerable convincing by the nursing staff to prevail on the mother to even accept her child back. Nan, in her straightforward and pragmatic way, conceived a simple solution that we used from then on in such circumstances. The next time we did this type of operation she brought the mother into the operating room with the baby and let her maintain physical contact with the child by holding its hand during the surgery. The mother was spared any view of the surgery by the simple expedient of walling her off with a drape.

The biblical scourge of leprosy continues to conjure visions of people hideously deformed; faces hidden by scarves and limbs rotting away; people relegated to a life of isolation, separated from society and loved ones. Indeed, for centuries leprosy patients were sequestrated from society in colonies, ministered to by brave doctors and nurses who devoted their lives to the treatment of this disease. Most leprosy patients are found in the Third World for reasons that are not altogether clear, but are thought by many to be related to poor hygiene and perhaps nutrition.

In fact, leprosy is an infectious disease. It is not easily spread from one person to another, although it is caused by a bacterium, a bacillus almost identical under a microscope to the bacillus of tuberculosis. It is known as Hansen's disease, named after the Norwegian researcher who discovered the bacillus. Many scholars believe that the description of leprosy in ancient documents such as the Bible was often tuberculosis, since the two are similar in many of the lesions that they cause. Only about ten percent of Caucasians are genetically susceptible to leprosy, which may explain the very low rate of contagion to those who care for patients with the disease. Long a scourge, recent statistics report that the number of people suffering from leprosy has fallen from 12.5 million to just 1.2 million in the last ten years. The reason for this decline is not altogether clear.

What does plastic surgery have to do with leprosy? The leprosy bacillus attacks the nerves, especially in the extremities and the face. Degeneration of the involved nerves occurs, eventually with paralysis of the muscles which are supplied by the affected nerves and/or loss of sensation to areas of skin. Thickening and grotesque growths of the skin occur when the bacillus invades the skin and subcutaneous tissues. These disabling deformities severely limit the patient's ability to work and to earn a living for the family. Reconstructive plastic surgery is able to improve or altogether correct the functional aspects of such deformities.

These characteristic deformities of the face identify the patient as a leper. The so-called "leonine" face resembles the face of a lion. Absence of fingers and toes and even hands and feet is the result of a loss of sensation (anesthesia) of the extremities. When sensation is lost, even a small wound such as a scratch or cut can become a major problem since the wound is likely to be neglected by the patient because it is not painful. Infection sets in, the wound or ulcer becomes larger and larger, and eventually the digits or limbs literally rot away.

Lepers have been cast out by society for centuries. Tragically, even after the disease is arrested by modern drug treatment, the patients often remain outcasts. Fewer patients nowadays develop the typical stigmata of leprosy. Education has resulted in early diagnosis and treatment of leprosy in many areas of the world. Hopefully, leprosy will soon be relegated to history, although recent evidence suggests that the bacillus is developing a resistance to the drugs used in therapy. Surgical reconstruction of the physical deformities becomes necessary when the disease is not arrested by medication or in patients with long-standing leprosy. Surgery is the key to restoration of function and returning the patient to a useful and productive life.

Our surgical schedule at Shirati included several operations performed on leprosy patients with paralysis of the muscles of the hands, feet, and face. Paralysis of certain muscles of the hand and forearm is devastating since it precludes the ability to perform even simple manual labor, such as holding a hammer, hoe or saw. An unsightly sagging of the lower eyelids can result in blindness caused by ulceration of the unprotected cornea. The paralyzed lid is unable to protect the cornea of the eye. During surgery, the paralyzed lid is suspended in order to protect the cornea. A strip of tendon or muscle is threaded around the eye opening, woven through the orbicularis oculi muscle (the muscle that closes the lids) and fixed by suture to a portion of the powerful temporalis muscle that closes the jaw. The patient learns to close his paralyzed eyelid by clenching his jaw.

Sagging from paralysis of the entire side of the face can be improved by a "face lift" and by suspending the paralyzed face with muscle transfers of unaffected muscles. Foot-drop is another disabling deformity associated with leprosy. Paralysis of the muscles that flex the ankle impairs the ability to walk without dragging the foot. Muscle transfers are useful to overcome foot-drop and support the paralyzed ankle muscles.

The operations useful in leprosy treatment are designed to redirect muscle pull by transferring healthy muscles that perform other functions to do the job of the paralyzed ones. The muscles that are transferred are more or less expendable, or at least their function can be shared with the paralyzed part. It is a medical example of "robbing Peter to pay Paul." Many of these procedures have become routine. They were pioneered by Dr. Paul Brand, a world-class expert on the surgery of leprosy. He worked out the dynamics of muscle and tendon transfers during his tenure as a missionary surgeon at Lahore Medical College in Pakistan. His techniques have been widely adopted throughout the world.

The leprosy colony at Shirati was a working model for a leprosy community. The patients and their families performed all the work in the community including farm work, building, maintenance, gardening and so forth. Everyone shared the responsibility for maintaining the community. The Mennonites' devotion to their patients, and the high level of medical care they provided, earned our profound respect and admiration. Their sense of cleanliness and orderliness was evident by the first-rate hospital they ran.

Few of the many hospitals that I have visited since have matched the standards of excellence of Shirati where an almost perfect symbiosis existed between the staff and the patients. The patients and their families were expected to contribute (i.e, to pay) in some way for the treatment of their family member. If money was not available, then the "bill" was paid by barter (chickens, for example) or by work on the farm or garden associated with the hospital. The patients, when well enough, or their families, were expected to feed and generally to look after the needs of the other patients as much as possible. This was especially true in the leprosy compound where patients often stayed for months or years. In this way everyone benefited—patients and hospital staff alike.

We left Shirati with a genuine sense of thankfulness for everything the staff there had accomplished and for the time we had shared with them. The old biblical concept of hospitality was never more evident at any bush hospital than at Shirati. The Mennonites truly lived their faith.

6

Arrow in the Chest

Our flight from Shirati to Kaimosi followed the eastern shore of Lake Victoria. The weather was clear and, as usual, Mike flew low to afford a close view of the terrain. We skimmed over the water, watching men casting their nets from ancient dugouts, and merchant boats plying their trade along the fertile coast. People along the shore waved at us as we flew overhead. The entire scene was spectacular and I got a sense of the vastness of Lake Victoria. In fact, everything about Africa seemed vast; just when you thought that nothing more could make an impression on you, a new and even grander vista would present itself and you would be lost again in wonder. As we traveled north Mike said that Kaimosi would be difficult to find. There were no navigational aids in the area to help us pinpoint the location. The hospital did have a radio to help guide us, but we would still need to have a good idea as to where we were in relation to the hospital, we only knew that a dirt road led to it.

As usual, Mike was entirely confident about his navigational skills. Men don't ask for directions, even in an airplane. When we got to where Mike thought the place should be, we flew round and round for an hour or so looking for the hospital buildings and the grass landing strip. I chided Mike constantly, which he took with good humor. But as the fuel gauge began to approach empty, he finally reckoned that we needed gas *now*. We changed course and flew to Kisumu, a good-sized town, easy to find, with a real airport. We landed and refueled. Mike talked with a pilot in the operations room and gained some helpful directions. Soon after take-off we located the outbuildings of Kaimosi and the dirt landing strip, barely visible from the air. Mike buzzed the compound as was the custom. As before, the strip was lined with children eagerly awaiting our landing. Mike brought us in and immediately shut off the engine the minute we were on the ground.

Kaimosi Hospital was managed by Dr. Peter Green, an energetic, workaholic hyperactive Englishman whom I was to see from time to time in subsequent East African travels. Whereas Dr. Eshleman had been the picture of piety and spoke in resonant, measured tones, Dr. Green, in rumpled khakis, looked like John Cleese on speed. He spoke in a rapid-fire, clipped, English Midlands accent. As we drove to the compound he gesticulated constantly, explaining the hospital operations: what was to be done, what had been done, where the patients came from and what the local traditions were. He was very enthusiastic about his job and clearly devoted to his patients whom he referred to as the *watu*, a Swahili word for people. Constantly under-funded, he was mildly critical of the mission sponsors in England; the standard complaint of almost all mission hospitals in Africa.

Peter greeted us warmly and was obviously glad to see us. Anticipating our visit, he had organized some interesting surgical cases for us to see. Patients with surgical problems had been called in from quite some distance around the hospital. A couple of the patients required general or orthopedic surgery—not our specialty—but he hoped we could help anyway, since the problems were beyond his capability and there was no general surgeon at Kaimosi at that time. We were comforted to hear that a capable nurse-anesthetist was in residence at the hospital. The good doctor invited us to begin our visit by joining him for lunch with his family, following which we would go on rounds.

Dr. Green's wife, Mary, was as energetic as he was—no small accomplishment. She was a wiry, intelligent woman who, as we subsequently came to appreciate, was an excellent manager, cook, housewife and teacher. She was also master of home remedies. For a day or so, Nan had been suffering a GI (gastrointestinal) upset. "You poor thing, a bit of 'gypi' tummy, eh? I'll give you a touch of the 'baby' and it will fix you right up," said Mary. "Baby", it turned out, was the "start" or activator for sour dough which she always kept fermenting on the back of the stove for just such occasions—as well as to make bread and biscuits. Like natural yogurt, sour dough is an excellent remedy for "TD" (traveler's diarrhea). It changes the bacterial flora of the large intestine, neutralizing the toxins. True to her promise, "baby" straightened Nan out within a few hours.

We spent what remained of the day (part of which we had lost by our inability to navigate directly to the airstrip) making rounds at the hospital and seeing candidate surgery patients in the outpatient clinic. The operating list included several cleft-lip and palate patients, burns to be grafted, a severe club foot (Mike was particularly interested in the surgery of club foot), a large vesico-vaginal fistula and an old woman who had sustained burns of the face, including the eyelids. The healed burn scars made it impossible for her to close her eyes and she was in danger of corneal ulceration and subsequent blindness. There was also a cosmetic breast reduction—something you wouldn't necessarily expect to be doing in a bush hospital—and an arrow wound of the chest (something you wouldn't expect to see in New York).

A vesico-vaginal fistula is a serious and not uncommon problem in Africa. As already mentioned in Chapter Four, it is an opening between the bladder and the vagina that results from prolonged and difficult labor without proper obstetrical care. When the baby's head pushes on the lower pelvis too long, the thin wall of tissue which separates the vagina from the bladder dies because the pressure stops the blood supply. The result is a hole (a fistula) between the bladder and the vagina. A loss of urinary control results with urine constantly pouring out of the vagina, a condition which frequently makes its victims subject to social ostracism. They are often abandoned by their husbands, as was the case with this patient.

A breast reduction of a very large, pendulous breast was scheduled on a young African woman. Enlargement (hypertrophy) of one breast but not the other is uncommon but by no means rare everywhere in the world. It was a real disaster for this patient. The enlargement occurred after puberty and after she was married. At the age of fifteen an important local chief had fallen in love with her and married her. She was the youngest and most beautiful, hence his favorite wife amongst five others. In his eyes, her beauty was marred only by the marked difference in the size of her breasts. Her right breast was at least twice the size of the left.

The chief regarded this transformation of one of her breasts as hideous. It had completely turned off his sexual appetite. She was in very real danger of losing her privileged status as the favored wife and might possibly be banished from his compound. Standards of beauty often cross cultural and social lines. I certainly never thought I would be performing a "cosmetic" breast reduction in the African bush. One might have thought that supposedly unsophisticated "bush" people would take such a condition in their stride; but that was not the case.

At surgery, I removed two-and-a-half pounds of breast tissue from the one large breast. To our surprise and amusement, the chief himself awaited us just outside the operating room door as we finished surgery and left the operating room for a cup of coffee. The bloody specimen of breast tissue was minutely examined by the chief and several of his relatives. Dr. Green explained that in this part of Africa it was customary for the next of kin to view any tissue removed during surgery, whether an appendix full of worms, or a breast or a uterus. It was believed that a special magic existed in surgical specimens, and that they should not be disposed of until seen by the family. According to belief, the size of the specimen often determined the success of the operation; hence an appendectomy is considered of little importance while two-and-a-half pounds of blood-smeared breast tissue was proof that an operation of great importance had taken place. The breast specimen impressed the chief, who said he was satisfied that the surgical *dawa* was indeed potent.

An arrow wound would prove to be a particular challenge. It seemed that a young warrior from a distant tribe had been shot in the chest with an arrow by a fellow tribesman who caught the victim in an adulterous act with his wife. Promiscuity was not uncommon in this particular tribe, but was best kept secret from the cuckolded husband. The wounded man had walked over twenty-five miles to the Kaimosi Hospital with the arrow protruding from his chest. He had lost a great deal of blood along the route and barely made it to the hospital a few days before we arrived. Immediately after his arrival, Dr. Green transfused him with two units of blood, and removed the arrow, but when he did, a gush of stomach contents escaped through the wound in his chest wall. A chest X-ray had showed that the arrow had passed through the lower lung, then through the diaphragm and into the stomach. A tunnel (fistula) had formed along the track of the arrow during the several days before its removal, through which the contents of the stomach (food and gastric juices) escaped to the outside of the chest wall. It was a miracle that the man survived the wound in the first place to say nothing of his long walk. He was destined to die of malnutrition unless the fistula could be closed and his normal alimentary tract re-established.

Mike and I were given the task of repairing the hole in his chest. Such an operation is fraught with problems because it requires opening the chest and the abdomen, repairing the damage and re-establishing the food passage from the esophagus to the stomach. There would be a lot of plumbing to deal with, and a lot of bone and connective tissue to get around. It would be a tricky, complicated procedure. The postoperative care would also be critical, to keep the lung from collapsing. Neither Mike nor I were chest surgeons, but we had been exposed to thoracic surgery during our general surgical training. We were the only hope the man had. Today, with our modern stretcher-bearing aircraft, we would have undoubtedly evacuated the patient to Kisumu or Nairobi, but such an option was not available to us then.

We set ourselves to the task, and everything went well. The arrow wound was very demanding; however, the resilient man survived, and so did we. The patient experienced a difficult recovery after surgery, but we later learned he eventually healed and was able to ingest food normally by mouth.

We treated the vesico-vaginal fistula by excising the scarred tract of the fistula and interspersing flaps of tissue from the vaginal wall on either side. I never learned whether the operation was successful in the long run in this particular woman. Operation for repair of vesico-vaginal fistula became much improved during the ensuing years so that today, a high degree of success is achieved by experienced surgeons.

At Kaimosi I first learned that rural people in some parts of Africa consider twins to be an evil omen and abandon them in the bush for hyenas and vultures to dispose of. While at Kaimosi, Nan and I joined in a frantic hunt in the bush for a pair of twins who had been born to a woman in a nearby village the night before. After hearing of the birth of these twins, Dr. Green immediately mobilized the entire staff of the hospital who searched every inch of the hospital compound and the surrounding bush in a desperate effort to find the babies before they were hidden and assigned to certain death. The twins were found in this instance and brought safely to the hospital compound. He told us that he had had a similar experience in the past that ended in tragedy because the twins were not found. The reason for abandoning twins to certain death in this way remains a mystery; also a paradox, for babies are much loved by African mothers. Infanticide is not limited to the African continent. Certain tribes in South America, such as the Uwa tribe in Colombia, customarily abandon twins in the forest or throw them into a lake. Nowadays, social workers and child rights advocates are working hard to reverse this ancient tradition.

Tired but energized by our work at Kiamosi, we flew to Nairobi and on to Mike's farm on Kilimanjaro for a weekend of R & R. The long-awaited three-day safari to the Ngorongoro Crater and Serengeti was soon to begin. The safari would be the beginning of a lifetime love affair with the natural world of Africa for Nan.

7

Elephant Hunter Extraordinaire

I was enjoying a cup of coffee after finishing the morning's operating schedule while I shed my operating pajamas for street clothes, when the chief operating room nurse at the Nairobi Hospital rapped on the door of the dressing room and peeked in. "Mr. Wood wants you to stop in the clinic on your way out," she said, "he has an interesting patient to show you." For some unknown reason, buried in tradition no doubt, it is the custom in England to address a surgeon who has passed the rigorous exams and become a Fellow of the Royal College of Surgeons, as "mister" instead of "doctor." It is a salutation of distinction throughout Britain, her colonies and the Commonwealth. Going from "Dr." to "Mr." seemed a retrograde step to me—I was so proud of my hard-earned "Doctor."

Anna, the head nurse of the clinic, met me at the outpatient clinic door, and ushered me into the consulting room, where I found Mike talking to an impressive-looking man. Deeply tanned, sandy-haired, about six feet two, perhaps weighing in the neighborhood of two hundred pounds. He was about forty years old. He resembled a somewhat diminished Arnold Schwartzenegger, with biceps the size of my thighs, a bull neck, and huge muscular calves and thighs. He was dressed in bush clothes—khaki shirt (with tufts of dark hair bursting forth from the collar), neatly pressed khaki shorts, a sleeveless bush vest, high calf socks and spit-polished leather chukka boots—a very rugged looking character indeed. I thought of Stewart Granger in *King Solomon's Mines*. Mike introduced him as Tony Adams (not his real name) from Arusha, in what was then Tanganyika. He conducted hunting safaris, specializing in trophy elephants.

As I wondered what kind of plastic surgery this quintessential representative of masculinity was interested in, Mike declared that Mr. Adams was requesting breast implants. His interest in the subject was stimulated by an article he had recently read in a woman's magazine about this relatively new operation (the year was 1958) that was rapidly gaining popularity with women throughout the Western world. Concealing my amazement, I asked him why he wanted to enlarge his breasts. He replied that for many years he had considered himself in every way, except anatomically, to be more female than male, but because of his profession and his marriage, he had suppressed the idea of having surgery to change his physical self to be more in tune with his emotional self and mental sexual orientation. He was experiencing increasing stress to become a physical woman. The desire to have surgery was becoming an obsession that he could no longer suppress.

I asked if his wife was aware of his plans and whether or not he had discussed having surgery with her. His wife, he said, was sympathetic and extraordinarily understanding, and had agreed not only to stay with him, but was willing to accept a homosexual relationship with him since he planned in the future to have a sex change operation. Breast augmentation was but a first step in his planned regime.

Sex change operations were rare in the US and England in the nineteen fifties. Cultural and psychological considerations were as yet poorly understood by the medical profession. Such surgery was generally frowned upon by the medical establishment, the majority of whom considered sex change surgery to be grotesque, even bordering on the unethical. Only a very few centers in America (such as Johns Hopkins University) had designed integrated programs with psychological evaluation and counseling as well as genetic studies, and investigation into ethical considerations. All parameters were taken into consideration before performing sex change surgery. Most patients gravitated to Scandinavia, particularly Denmark, where a more enlightened attitude prevailed. The technique necessitates complicated plastic surgery including amputation of the penis and reconstruction of a vagina with skin grafts. Fearing possible legal action as well as disapproval from colleagues, most surgeons were reluctant to perform such surgery.

Mr. Adams reminded me that Sir Harold Gillies (famed for his pioneering role in developing the specialty during World War I) was intrigued by the technical challenge of sex change. Preferring not to do the surgery in England for reasons alluded to above, he operated from time to time in India where attitudes were more favorable.

Tony, who requested a first name relationship, hoped to arrange for Sir Harold to do the surgery in India at a subsequent time, but wanted breast augmentation first, a less drastic but logical place to start his odyssey. After researching on his own the various methods of augmenting the breast, he had decided on surgical breast augmentation rather than female hormone therapy. Estrogen therapy resulted in feminizing consequences such as loss of body hair, elevation of voice pitch and female fat distribution which he was not yet prepared to accept. Additionally, in the unlikely possibility that he would at some point wish to reverse the process, he reasoned that breast implants could be removed.

Enlargement of the breasts with free grafts of fat and skin from the buttocks, was the only surgical technique in use prior to the development of polyvinyl plastic sponge. Fat-skin grafts from the buttocks also reduced the size of the buttocks while increasing the size of the breasts, but often left unsightly scars on the donor area of the buttocks. Unfortunately, these skin-fat grafts were absorbed within a year or so leaving only scar tissue and no breast enlargement. A new era of breast enlargement began with the manufacture of the industrial plastic sponge. The poor long-term results of sponge implants eventually culminated in the development of the various silicone implants widely used in succeeding years.

I explained the complications and untoward results that could result from the procedure to Tony, at the same time trying to keep my eyes from wandering to his chest, and wondering how his hunting clients would interpret enlarged breasts on their "white hunter." Since the surgery was relatively new, I emphasized that the long-term results were unknown, and that there might be other problems as yet undiscovered. Despite my lecture, Tony remained adamant in his desire to have breasts. He agreed to sign a document indicating that he understood that complications could result from the surgery and absolving Mike and me from legal actions that might result. A second consultation was prudently arranged to discuss any other details that might have been overlooked during the first and to bring his wife into the picture as much as possible.

Mike and I were curious as to what his wife's reaction was to this most unusual step. We wanted to hear it first hand from her. We also wanted to explore her relationship with her husband in view of his declaration that they would eventually live together as lesbians following the proposed sex change surgery. Psychiatric evaluation was not available in Nairobi in 1958, so that his wife's evaluation of his mental status and "reality quotient" became of utmost importance. She confirmed that Tony had persisted in his desire to become a female for a long time. In the hope of keeping the family intact (they had two children), she had agreed to a lesbian relationship with him. She insisted that she loved him and concurred with his plan to eventually undergo a full sex change operation.

A second consultation with Tony confirmed what we had learned at the first. Mike and I agreed to perform the surgery as soon as I could have some polyvinyl sponge air expressed from New York. During spare moments, we discussed Tony's case at length, exploring every ramification and detail of it. We debated the pros and cons of the ethics involved over and over again. There were no other plastic surgeons or psychiatrists in Nairobi for us to consult with.

We were convinced that he was not psychotic, an important determination in sex change cases, for mental illness could result in disaster for us all, doctors and patient alike. More than one plastic surgeon has been killed by mentally disturbed male patients after operations that were interpreted as sexually threatening. To the mentally disturbed, the nose can represent the penis, so that operations on the nose in such a patient can have disastrous effects; likewise, operation on the genitalia such as circumcision can elicit exaggerated fears of castration. In some instances, surgery has tipped a borderline emotional disorder into a full-blown psychosis. However, except for his desire to become a woman, we found Tony to be as "normal" as apple pie. Facetiously, between ourselves, we referred to him as "Tonina." A touch of humor, but in no way meant to disparage him.

Preparations began the night before surgery. We meticulously sculpted the shape of a female breast from a square block of polyvinyl sponge. Allowing for the normal shrinkage of at least fifty percent, our goal was to achieve a B cup size, despite the patient's emphatic request for more. We reasoned that a B cup stood a reasonable chance of being camouflaged beneath a loose bush vest.

Content with the size and shape, we boiled the implant for thirty minutes, well beyond the ordinary ten minutes usually recommended for sterilization. The implant was then placed in a sterile polyethylene bag filled with penicillin solution. Postoperative infection was the most common complication following the implantation of sponge implants. The porous nature of the sponge provided a fluid-filled environment in which bacteria could easily propagate. Such low-grade infections frequently resulted in the formation of sinus tracts: tunnels from the implant through to the surface of the skin through which pus drained. Infected sponges were difficult to treat, even with intensive antibiotics. Infected implants eventually became exposed, necessitating their removal.

Even when infection set in, many women were reluctant to have their breast implants removed, an indication of the importance ascribed to a "normal" sized breast. In my practice in New York I had seen a number of women with infected sponge implants who, despite the inconvenience of continual drainage from sinus tracts, steadfastly refused to have them removed until the nuisance of constantly changing pus-soaked dressings, sometimes several times each day, finally convinced them that removal was the only logical solution to the problem.

Improved technology and material eventually replaced the early polyurethane sponge implants with silicone gel and later saline-filled silicone implants. Infection became a rare complication. We were determined to do everything in our power to avoid infection in Tony, hence the boiling "overkill" and soaking the sponges in penicillin. We also administered large does of penicillin before, during, and for several days after the operation.

Shrinkage of the implants with considerable loss of volume was the norm with sponge implants. The body, attempting to isolate and wall off foreign material, produced scar tissue, which invaded the implants which then solidified. Scar tissue contracts with time, so that once infiltrated with scar, the sponges would undergo shrinkage. Sometimes only a small rock hard lump was the final result.

The operation went smoothly and the postoperative course was uneventful. "Tonina" was discharged from the hospital and returned to the wilds of Tanganyika and a career of elephant hunting. Mike wrote to me in New York several weeks later to report that our patient had healed very well with no evidence of late infection. He had returned to his profession of hunting and to his family.

I lost track of Tony for several years, until he showed up in Mike's clinic in Nairobi during one of my working trips to Africa. He complained of firmness and shrinkage of his breasts. He had indeed gone to India where Sir Harold Gillies had performed a sex change operation. Sir Harold had amputated his penis and testicles and used the skin of his scrotum as lining for a vagina which he constructed by making a space between the bladder and the rectum. Part of the scrotal lining skin had not survived and Sir Harold had replaced it with a free skin graft from Tony's thigh.

Tony considered the operation to be a great success. The reconstructed vagina accepted a dildo during intercourse with his wife. He even claimed to achieve orgasm. I had not been exposed to anyone who had sex change surgery before and had no way of evaluating the truth of what Tony claimed. On the other hand I had no reason to disbelieve him especially since his wife (who was present) confirmed what he said. He was also still guiding big game hunting safaris and had not heard a comment from any of his clients about the size of his breasts.

By this time the new generation of silicone implants developed by Dr. Tom Cronin of Texas was available. Mike and I removed the sponges, a difficult task because of the extensive scar tissue. We replaced the sponges with the current generation of silicone gel implants. His recovery was smooth and he returned to Tanganyika which in the meantime had become Tanzania with the advent of independence. I never heard of Tony again, despite sporadic efforts to find him. Somewhere in Tanzania there may still be a rugged elephant-hunting guide, posing in the guise of a man.

8

An Encounter with the Maasai

On one of my working trips to Africa, Nan and I took our nine-year-old son Tommy along to acquaint him with the country he had heard so much about from us. At the completion of my working safari in which I had visited four bush hospitals with a surgical team, we took some time off from our working schedule. Enjoying a few days rest for sightseeing, we stopped at Keekorok Game Lodge in the Maasai Mara game reserve in Kenya. Keekorok Lodge commands a magnificent view of the savannah. Thousands of animals can be seen passing by during the migration. Our friends the Block family owned the lodge, which was comfortable, and the food was excellent, too.

On this particular visit we went on a game run the first afternoon in a Land Rover borrowed from the lodge and driven by Stephen, an African guide. Prides of lions, herds of Cape buffalo and elephant, numerous topi, eland, kongoni, hyenas, warthogs, plus a solitary leopard, and a host of other animals thrilled and delighted our son. Three cow elephants took offense at our proximity to their calves and with trunks in the air charged the car, trumpeting triple fortissimo with their great ears flapping. Tom screamed with pleasure (or fright) as they stopped short of our car, by fifty feet or so. "They are just trying to scare us away, it was a false charge," explained Stephen.

We arrived back fairly late and, after a shower, enjoyed an evening drink on the veranda, watching animals at a waterhole right in front of the lodge. Dinner was delicious and very welcome after the long day. A succulent steak had an unusual but tasty flavor. We learned, to our surprise, that the steak was zebra, and that it had been marinated in Coca Cola, an excellent method of tenderizing wild game meat. The lodge chef said that Coke contains enzymes and sugar that break down the tough protein fibers of game meat. Reliving the exciting elephant charge of that afternoon over a cup of coffee, we were joined by Mrs. Lasse Allan, the lodge manager with whom we discussed our plans for the remainder of our stay.

We spent the next day exploring, once more with Stephen, allowing Tommy to get acquainted with the area and its wildlife. Back at the lodge after an early tea that afternoon, Mrs. Allan asked if I would be good enough to talk with the local game warden Ole Tipis. She said that he was an excellent warden, a Maasai originally from the local area. She knew that I was one of the founders of the Flying Doctors. I had met her previously with Mike Wood, when I had prescribed medication to treat her for a severe case of gastroenteritis. She credited me with curing her problem and had been grateful ever since. I said that I would be happy to meet with Mr. Tipis, and suggested that he stop by our room. Mrs. Allan said that Mr. Tipis was waiting by her office and that she would bring him round to see me.

In just a few moments she was back with a tall, handsome African in a khaki uniform, wearing the insignia of a Kenya game warden. He had an intelligent face and a direct manner. I immediately liked him. His handshake was firm and confident. I noticed that he had the characteristic ear lobe perforations of a Maasai moran; however, the beaded adornments were absent in accordance with his new position in society. Probably his beads and jewelry had to be jettisoned with his blanket and spear. I wondered if he resented having to make this sacrifice of traditional jewelry and weapons. It's too bad, I thought, that people have to give up so much of their heritage just to fit in to what we expect in the West.

Speaking excellent English with just a touch of African accent, Mr. Tipis asked to be excused for intruding on our safari, but said he had a problem and needed the advice of a doctor. He was not sure whether his problem was serious or not. With his limited medical training, he wanted a consultation before involving the authorities on a matter that might affect many Maasai in the area. He did not want to sound a false alarm or unnecessarily stir up a hornets' nest. I indicated that I would be glad to help in any way I could, and asked what the problem was.

Mr. Tipis said that there were several Maasai *manyattas* on the edge of the Mara Reserve, and that some of them were inside the reserve boundaries—although it was against the law and conflicted with their agreement with the government. He reminded us that most of the Maasai were nomads who followed the rains, seeking water and fresh grass for their cattle. The Maasai, he said, considered the Maasai Mara Game Reserve as belonging to them, just as American Indians claim much of the West as their own.

He said that a *moran* had visited him that morning along with his son, who looked about eight years old. The *moran* claimed that the boy had been sick for about two or three weeks, too sick to herd the goats. He had been spending most of the day sleeping in their hut. The *moran* had shown Mr. Tipis open sores on the boy's scalp which alarmed the game warden, who had recently attended a lecture given by the Game Department about various diseases that they might encounter in nomads and their animals. The lecture had focused on anthrax as a disease that affects both cattle and sometimes humans. Mr. Tipis had never seen anything like this amongst the Maasai in all the years he had lived in the traditional way, or since. On questioning, the *moran* denied that any of his cattle were sick, but the game warden worried that an epidemic might be just beginning. He asked me to please accompany him to the *manyatta*, examine the boy and give an opinion as to whether his illness could be anthrax. The father had agreed to bring his boy, and meet us at the bridge over the Mara River, just outside the reserve.

I asked if it would be all right if I brought my son to the meeting since he was about the same age, and I hoped he might learn from the encounter. Mr. Tipis agreed that it might be a good idea in that it could allay the Maasai youngster's fears at meeting with a white *daktari*.

We climbed into Mr. Tipis's Land Rover and were off on the road to the reserve boundary. The road was good and we arrived in a short time at a bridge spanning the Mara River. A Maasai man stood with a boy at his side. The man was splendid. He was draped in a red blanket and stood with spear and stick in hand. His hair was plastered with ochre and mud swept back to a kind of pony tail. Ivory hoops dangled from one earlobe. A can of snuff inserted into the large hole in his other earlobe. His sandals appeared to be of skin and rope. He wore a beaded necklace with some metal figure as a pendant. Around his wrists and ankles were twisted copper bracelets. He was lean and tall with the characteristic handsome Nilotic face of a pure Maasai. His son appeared somewhat emaciated, although the line between emaciated and lean is fine with these people. Maasai are thin until they eat rich carbohydrate urban food. Their traditional diet consists of curdled milk, cattle blood and meat, and various fruits and berries from the bush. Both father and son exuded a kind of arrogance so characteristic of their tribe. By inference, it was clear that they considered us to be inferior beings.

Ole Tipis and the man began an intense conversation. I strained to hear any Swahili words that I might understand, but the conversation was entirely in Maasai. Interpreting for me, Ole asked that I be allowed to examine the man's son. He explained that I was a very important *mgunga* (doctor) with strong *dawa* (medicine) that might cure his son's illness. Apparently there was no objection, for Ole Tipis signaled me to go ahead and examine the boy. Tommy stood in the background, fascinated with his first close-up view of two Maasai males, one in the prime of manhood and the other a boy of his own age. He must have wondered what this young Maasai did to amuse himself other than herd cattle and goats. He certainly would never play soccer, ski or ride a surfboard.

The Maasai boy with his shaved head, wooden plugs dilating each earlobe and clad only in a rag of a blanket and sandals was a sharp contrast to my son—far more than that dictated by the difference in the color of their skins. The Maasai lived a nomadic life in temporary huts made of bent sticks covered with mud and cow dung. This boy, with no permanent home, traveled constantly as the "village" moved in search of fresh grass and water. He would be circumcised into manhood as a teenager in a traditional tribal ceremony. When he grew up he could enjoy sex with the wife of any member of his circumcision group, which could be quite large, sometimes numbering over one thousand women. To have sex with the wife of any man outside of his circumcision brothers meant severe punishment; death in the old days. Sex was to be enjoyed—no guilt attached. But also a life without ice cream, Cokes, Big Macs, movies, TV shows, baseball games, and rock concerts.

His life would be constantly threatened by a multitude of illnesses including malaria, venereal disease, enterocolitis, parasites and infections almost unknown in the West. There was only a small chance that such a boy could acquire a higher education, unless he became one of the few singled out by government or missionary schools to be educated. Neither was there much chance of acquiring material wealth as we in the "civilized" world know it. Cattle constitute the only wealth that a Maasai values. Cattle are the main source of food and principal means of trade and barter. Of course, as the Maasai become more integrated into modern African society, these values have begun to change.

I examined the youth carefully. Open, seeping, crusted sores covered his scalp. These were clearly infected and badly in need of a clean up. I could feel several lumps in his neck, probably enlarged lymph nodes. My knowledge of anthrax was scanty to say the least. I had never seen a case, but I dimly remembered from my medical school studies that the disease can cause open sores like this in humans, the so-called cutaneous form of the disease. I remembered that enlarged lymph nodes in the neck were characteristic of anthrax.

82

Anthrax has been long feared by health officials as a potential biological weapon way before the actual use of this bacterium became a reality in the United States. Anthrax is an infection easily spread in the so-called weapon form in which the spores are milled down into exceedingly fine particles smaller than six microns in size. Such "weapons grade anthrax" easily passes through ordinary mail envelopes or through air conditioning systems in buildings.

The anthrax bacillus has a unique characteristic appearance under a microscope, where it appears as a small rod. The bacillus produces spores which are very resistant to destruction, remaining viable in soil and animal products for decades, and capable of causing infection in both humans and ruminants. Human infection usually occurs through direct contact, passing through the skin or following ingestion of contaminated meat. Pulmonary anthrax results from inhaling spores from an infected animal, and could be spread by a biological weapon. The pulmonary form of the disease is highly dangerous and usually fatal unless vigorously treated early in the course of the infection with massive doses of penicillin.

The skin (cutaneous) form of anthrax begins as a reddish-brown hard pimple that enlarges with an area of redness surrounding it. Eventually, this lump grows and erupts into a blister which in turn ulcerates and exudes pus. Such a lesion is then easily spread to other areas of the skin by the victim's fingers having been contaminated with the pus. Local lymph nodes are frequently involved, forming hard lumps that can be palpated through the skin. Generalized symptoms include severe headache, nausea and vomiting and flu-like symptoms. The skin eruptions are technically not contagious but can be spread by direct contact from an infected skin lesion to a healthy person with the ability of spreading quickly through a small community such as a Maasai village.

Anthrax is primarily a disease of cattle, but can easily spread from cows to people. I knew that whole herds of cattle had to be destroyed when anthrax struck, imposing a severe economic burden on the owners. I couldn't rule it out in this boy. This could possibly be anthrax, but with my flimsy knowledge, I needed definitive laboratory findings. The boy could have a myriad of other diseases to account for the sores, including plain impetigo (staph infection) of the scalp. I realized the tough spot Ole Tipis was in. If it was truly anthrax it could mean that the cattle were likely to be infected, or would be—a catastrophe for the Maasai. I was not sure what the implications were for the wild animals of the Maasai Mara.

I told Mr. Tipis that I was not at all sure what the sores on the boy represented, but that I certainly understood his predicament. I suggested that we drive him and his father to the nearest government or missionary clinic and try to get a diagnosis. We needed a culture of those sores at once. He responded that he would try to convince them, but thought that there was a very slim chance that the man would agree since he had refused this opportunity even before my arrival on the scene. Now that the boy had been examined by a doctor which might have given credence to his suggestion, Ole was going to try again.

A long and intense conversation followed between Ole Tipis and the Maasai herdsman. Ole reported that the *moran* absolutely refused to let us take the boy to a clinic—it was unthinkable even though we informed him that the boy might die unless he got proper treatment. I thought this rather dire prediction might win our argument. More discussion followed, with the pace of the negotiations picking up.

Summarizing the conversation, Ole Tipis told me that the man told him that it did not matter if the boy died since we all die sometime. The Maasai do not regard death with the dread that most other people do. Death is not considered especially terrible. It is a natural process in their eyes. They also believe that, like their ancestors, they return as flies. They simply do not worry about it. "What will be will be." Said Ole Tipis.

I was now perplexed. If this was anthrax and we let the boy return to the *manyatta*, he might well spread it to others—if he hadn't already. These lesions (sores) looked as though they could easily contaminate others, but how was I going to persuade this man to let us get the boy to medical care? "Tell him that if the boy has a bad disease, all of his cattle might get it and they will die." I said. I thought this was a stroke of sheer genius on my part since I knew how the Maasai feel about their cattle.

With this bit of information, the Maasai gasped. It was clear that we had his attention at last. Humans are one thing, but cattle are another (and much more important)! The loss of cattle is serious stuff indeed. Despite his concern, however, we could not budge him. During these negotiations my son was following the proceedings with great interest. This was beyond his nine-year-old comprehension. How anyone could refuse an offer of proper medical treatment when they were sick was a mystery to Tom. Like any Western boy, my son was trotted off to the doctor at the slightest hint of illness. Here was an African boy with horrendous looking sores and scabs all over his scalp whose father would not permit treatment.

As a final desperate effort to save the day, I asked Ole Tipis to persuade the man to bring his son back the next morning to meet us. I would have culture tubes flown out from Nairobi at first light and at least see if we could grow anthrax bacilli out of the sores. With much convincing by Mr. Tipis, the *moran* reluctantly agreed to return with the boy as long as we promised not to take him away. Not exactly triumphant, but hopeful that we had an alternative, we returned to Keekorok. Using the radio at lodge headquarters, I called Flying Doctors radio control. I explained the situation in somewhat guarded tones, never mentioning the word anthrax to avoid alarming eavesdroppers (radio communication frequencies are not private). I requested, as a high priority, that one of our planes drop off some bacterial culture media tubes first thing in the morning.

The nurse on radio duty was inquisitive and wanted to know what was so important that it warranted sending a plane all the way to Keekorok just to deliver culture tubes when there was no patient to evacuate. I asked her to please take my word for it, that it was indeed very important, and that the plane was to return with the cultures for examination by the lab at the Nairobi Hospital. Fortunately, a plane was already scheduled for a trip to Mwanza in Tanzania early the next morning, and its route passed almost directly over the Mara where we were. The nurse promised to arrange for some culture tubes to be delivered to us en route and to be picked up later on the plane's return to Nairobi.

I was greatly relieved by this solution to our problem, hoping that we could meet with the boy in the morning, culture his sores, and have the cultures ready for pick-up by the plane on its return from Mwanza.

The story ended in disappointment in the morning. We returned to the rendezvous spot. Not only had the boy and his father disappeared, but the entire village had moved, leaving behind an empty manyatta. For the next month, we watched apprehensively for any news of an outbreak of anthrax amongst the Maasai or their livestock in Kenya or Tanzania. Fortunately, an epidemic did not materialize. How could I have persuaded this father to trust me enough to draw a blood specimen from his son? What else could we have done to convince him of the possible danger of the sores on his son's head? How could I have imparted to him the danger to his cattle if the disease proved to be anthrax? How could I assure him that the nomadic life he cherished was not in jeopardy? To obtain the cooperation of people whose culture and traditions are far different from our own depends so much on understanding how to communicate.

This small drama when my son was nine years old has often been the subject of conversation with him over the ensuing years. He always wondered what happened to the Maasai boy with sores on his head. I wish that I knew too. Ole Tipis, our game warden, went on to a distinguished career in politics. I have not seen him since.

9

A Place of Peace

Rising high above the plains of northern Tanzania, the Ngorongoro Crater, the largest unbroken caldera on earth, often called the eighth wonder of the world, stands like a giant jewel reaching to the sky. Covered with rain forest, the steep-walled rim, fifty miles around the top, rises two thousand feet above the crater floor. A savannah, rich in grasslands and containing both fresh and soda lakes, covers the floor of the crater. Inside is an ecosystem containing tens of thousands of birds and some 25,000 large mammals. A wide spectrum of animal species was found there, including elephant, zebra, buffalo, hippo, rhino, several different gazelle species, and other plains game. As though contained in a huge open zoo, these animals graze in clusters all over the floor of the crater. The rich food resources attract lions, hyenas, and predators of all kinds.

In 1978 we were on safari with Tor Allan, an old friend and arguably the best safari guide in East Africa. Our party, in addition to Tor, included David Niven, Jr., Donald and Hillary McPherson, personal friends from London, my wife Nan and myself, and Barufa, Tor's long-time game tracker. Tor was driving one car, a Range Rover converted into a safari car. I was driving the other, a Toyota Land Cruiser. We traveled in tandem.

The narrow, precipitous car track snaked its way down the inner face of the crater wall to the floor below. A blanket of cloud covered the rim in the early morning. A mist obscured the floor. Numerous switchbacks plagued our descent. At times, the wheels of our safari car came perilously close to the edge of a sheer drop, hundreds of feet down. It was a breathtaking and heart-stopping ride. Negotiating this treacherous road required my undivided attention. Despite having logged many thousands of miles in off-road vehicles in remote areas, I was a bit tense with the responsibility of driving passengers new to bush travel.

The Land Cruiser safari car was not new. The brakes were worn and the gears much stiffer than I was used to. The track was negotiated in a compound low ratio gear. Missing a gear at the wrong moment could send us plunging into space. My passengers that morning kept their fears to themselves as we crept down the track with frequent grinding of gears.

Heavy cloud embraced us for the first part of the descent. Small beads of moisture covered the car. The imagined hazards of the drive were magnified with our visibility limited to only a few feet. But as we continued, the morning sun began to burn shafts of light through the cloud as we descended ever closer to the bottom. From time to time we were rewarded with glimpses of what awaited us below. The view intensified our anticipation of a great day in the crater.

On reaching the floor, the cars separated, but kept in contact by radio. A thrilling adventure awaited us. To wander through herds of wild animals is an exhilarating experience unlike any other. An element of danger thrills the imagination. Surprise can come from any quarter and the unexpected is usual. Reading about wild game or seeing it on TV cannot convey the excitement of being just a few feet from an agitated elephant or a pride of lions feeding on a carcass.

The photo opportunities during the game run that morning proved to be exceptional. The resident animals and birds of the crater put on a splendid show capped by a rhino charge. Tor had developed, with much practice, what he euphemistically called a "rhino mating call"; basically a high-pitched squeal. Despite the fact that this ridiculous sound attracted rhinos, it is unlike any sound I have ever heard from a human. This morning, showing off, I believe, Tor bleated at a large black rhino male who glowered malevolently at us for a minute or two, and then charged straight at Tor's car. Deft piloting on Tor's part managed to avoid a collision and the rhino galloped off after a near miss, tail in the air. Aside from some shaken passengers, no harm was done.

By prearrangement we met for lunch at a favorite picnic spot in a clearing with a commanding view of the crater floor. The midday sun is hot in Ngorongoro, so the shade provided by two large baobab trees and several acacias provided a welcome respite. It was a good place for a picnic, and perhaps a short snooze.

As we were arranging our lunch and sipping a cool drink, a safari car with "Ker & Downey Safaris" printed on each door, pulled up under a nearby tree. I recognized the guides as David Jones and his wife Faith. David was a veteran guide from the days of hunting safaris. When hunting in Kenya was outlawed, David, like many others, turned to photographic safaris. His wife, Faith, was a sought after safari guide in her own right, with wide experience. She is the antithesis of what one would expect of a woman safari guide: attractive and soft spoken but expert in the ways of the back country. Tough and "bush wise" with an expert knowledge of East Africa, the Joneses were popular with clients for their pleasant dispositions and caring attitudes. The two often teamed up when more than one guide was required on an expedition.

They unloaded a wheelchair from the back of the safari car. Then, with considerable exertion, transferred a woman from the back seat into the wheelchair. Although it was not obvious what her problem was, the woman was clearly disabled. With limited motor ability and little strength, it was difficult for her to help the guides to negotiate the transition from car to wheelchair. She was elderly, in her seventies I guessed. Her face was round, the bone structure ill-defined, and her cheeks and eyelids appeared swollen and puffy. Edema, I guessed, possibly from steroid therapy or heart disease, maybe kidney problems. Her chest heaved in and out rapidly with shallow excursions and she gasped slightly, clutching noticeably for each breath. Tinged with a purplish color, her skin was pasty looking, changing in hue as she struggled to breathe.

I marveled that a woman of her age and condition was off in the middle of Tanzania. What incredible motivation she must have for enduring such an uncomfortable, and for her, potentially catastrophic journey in a hard-sprung safari car over some of the roughest pot-holed roads in the world. While unfair, comparing people that I encounter while traveling with those that I see in my medical practice in New York is an irrepressible habit of mine.

Observing her determination, brought to mind a finicky patient in New York I had seen on several visits just before coming to Africa who was bitching endlessly about a slight thickening in the scars behind her ear from a recent facelift. I could not help but wonder how she would have reacted if she found herself sick and traveling in the wilds of Africa without a husband, and with limited comforts available. Whatever reason brought this courageous woman here in the heart of the bush certainly was convincing proof that limitations imposed by a failing body can be endured, even overcome, by a compelling motivation.

What on earth was an experienced safari company like Ker & Downey thinking of, taking a woman so ill on a tented safari in Tanzania? My natural medical curiosity was ignited. Considerable effort was required to suppress my desire to introduce myself and ask some obvious medical questions. I sensed that it would be considered intrusive. Besides, I reasoned, the Joneses would ask my opinion if they were seriously worried about her immediate health. I was not well enough acquainted with either of them to barge into their client's affairs. Concerned, I kept a watchful eye on her during lunch seeking some clue as to the identity of her illness. A woman traveling companion was very attentive to her every need.

Although we enjoyed separate picnics, some small talk and comparing of game sightings was shared by our two parties. Faith Jones introduced the ill woman as Mrs. Porter from Del Ray Beach, Florida, and Boston. Her labored breathing and obvious discomfort concerned me more and more. I fought my urge to interfere, although logic told me that it probably would not change anything. Her illness was too advanced even then. I later found out that she had really lost her desire to live—for reasons that we shall see.

Some things are meant to be: fate, karma, maybe. Several times in my medical career I have had similar experiences, glimpses of fate, premonitions. Many doctors have comparable experiences. Sometimes there is a perception that no matter how expert the treatment, it is going to fail in a patient who really does not possess strong will and determination. My intuition at that lunch told me that this woman was not going to live much longer.

My experience, made richer by my extensive travels in the Third World, persuaded me to trust my intuition, that important sixth sense. Good doctors have a power of making intuitive diagnoses. They can "smell" a serious disease. It does not necessarily help the power of healing. The ability to intuitively perceive bodily imbalance (disease) is an ancient art in India. Indian physicians aid their intuition by feeling the pulse. The Western doctor often believes in the importance of the laying-on of hands. These tactile contacts with the patient provide a vehicle for intensifying communication between doctor and patient. Perhaps a flow of power, a tactile telepathy, a direct pathway between patient and healer is established.

Any surgeon knows that it is a reasonable bet that a patient about to enter the operating room who expresses the strong conviction that he or she is not going to survive the operation, often does not. It always scares the hell out of surgeons and anesthetists when a patient is convinced that he or she is going to die.

Our parties separated after lunch, each going its separate way. As the afternoon faded, the cars clawed their way back up the narrow track to the crater rim, descending down the outer wall of the crater to the Serengeti Plain. Our destination was Ndutu, a permanent safari camp in the Southeast sector of the Serengeti. Located very near a river and several small lakes, Ndutu lies in the path of the wildebeest migration. Ndutu enjoys a strategic location; convenient for sorties into the surrounding plain to see the animals of the Serengeti, and to follow the progress of the migration. Many miles of intense searching is required to find the scattered game when the migration moves on. An airstrip about a mile from the main camp was maintained in good condition, and used to ferry supplies and people to and from the Serengeti.

During the drive from Ngorongoro to Ndutu, a beautiful pair of cheetahs, an adult female and a yearling, suddenly emerged from the thorn acacia trees and scrub brush along the road. When hunting, cheetahs are not particularly shy about the presence of humans, but it was unusual to see them ambling along quite unconcerned, directly abreast of the vehicle containing the Joneses and their client. They kept next to the car for two or three miles, not hunting, just moving on with their loping gait. Nan remarked, "It looks as though they have come out to greet Mrs. Porter and her party." The two cheetahs vanished into the bush as suddenly as they had arrived as the buildings of the camp came into view. David Jones later told me that the disabled woman was quite taken with this female cheetah and her cub. She speculated that she had lost her mate and was all alone in the world, an idea that saddened her.

A series of small cottages all in a row endows Ndutu with the appearance of an old-fashioned motel in the States. The furnishings are "Africa rustic", the bathrooms and showers a bit primitive but essentially clean and comfortable (as bush camps in Africa go). A separate building with a large pleasant terrace serves as the main dining room and bar. Other buildings serve as administrative headquarters, service rooms, staff quarters, generator housing and the like. In the evening before dinner, the guests at Ndutu customarily gather on the terrace next to the bar to enjoy a sundowner. That evening, David and Faith and their two clients joined us as we ordered our drinks.

Mrs. Porter was obviously in more distress than she had been at lunch in the Crater. Her skin color was now definitely cyanotic, a deeper blue-purple, interrupted with patterned blotches of ashen paleness. She was breathing in short cadence, sucking in as much air with each gasp as the shallow excursion of her chest wall would allow. With each breath, the veins of her neck became distended. I looked at her more closely and noticed that she had the typical barrel-chest configuration of emphysema. Betraying edema, the back of her hands and ankles were puffy. What a game lady, I thought.

I could only imagine what she must be suffering. Surely she must be afraid, in such distress and so far from any medical facility of the type she would be used to. She made a valiant effort to conceal her distress and to exude cheerfulness. Her shortness of breath did not prevent her from having a cigarette with her Scotch and soda. I wondered if it was the "it doesn't make any difference now anyway" attitude that so many people adopt when in the grip of a chronic disease.

"Faith, tell me about this lady," I discreetly asked. Faith told me that she was a wonderful woman. She thought she was in her late seventies. Her husband had died recently, and she had come out to East Africa to spread his ashes over the Maasai Mara in Kenya. It was his final instruction to her. They had been married for over fifty years; a real love match. Faith said that she talked of little else but what a wonderful and full life she'd had with him. They had loved to travel and went all over the world together. The year before he died, they took their last trip together—a safari in Kenya. They fell completely in love with Africa like so many first-time visitors do. They saw the tail end of the migration in the Mara. This taste of the migration made them want to return and see the main event in the Serengeti. He died before they could fulfill their dream. She had come determined to see it now for the both of them.

I was resolved to find out more about her condition. I moved my chair closer to Mrs. Porter and putting on all the charm I could muster, tried to draw her out. All to no avail. She was pleasant and conversational but evaded my attempts to discover what her symptoms were. Thinking about her, I tried to put myself in her position. God knows, if my wife pledged me to bring her ashes to East Africa, I would do so. But I did wonder if I would continue on safari to fulfill a dream shared with my wife, just to see the migration if I were as sick as this woman so clearly was. Not suffering as she was and having no way of personally assuming her burden of ill health, I couldn't decide what I would do under the circumstances.

Our two groups separated at dinner, each to its own table. Afterwards, weary from the long day, we retired early to our rooms. Soon, David and Faith knocked on my door. Swearing me to professional confidence, they asked me as a doctor to help out if her situation worsened. David was very concerned that his client was getting in a bad way. I believed she was now deteriorating fast. She could be heard coughing and wheezing in her room. The Joneses had looked in, but Mrs. Porter insisted that she was okay and wished to be left alone. Faith thought that she'd been going downhill fast ever since they'd left Arusha three days before. They noticed that she had become increasingly short of breath on the climb up to the rim of the Crater. This evening at dinner Mrs. Porter had said that for the first time in her life her evening drink and cigarette tasted "off."

I asked them why they would take someone in such poor health on safari anyway? The altitude in Nairobi alone is getting on for six thousand feet, a real burden for a cardiac patient. I pointed out that the top of the Ngorongoro Crater was eight thousand feet in elevation—an even worse place for a sick person with oxygen starvation. "We know Tom," Faith said, "her doctor advised us beforehand that she has a heart problem and emphysema. She has also had both breasts removed for cancer. We were naturally very concerned about it, but before the trip she sent a signed waiver drawn up by her lawyer and a disclaimer of all responsibility as far as Ker & Downey is concerned. Her own doctor in the States urged us to take her. Her companion on this trip is supposed to be a nurse." Faith was very worried that something might happen during the night, specifically that she might die.

"Why don't you insist that I see her now," I asked. "I would think that as her guides you have some right to do so." "She won't have any of it," said David. "I think she knows she is going to die and does not want anyone to interfere. She told us tonight that seeing the herds of animals today in the Serengeti on the way to Ndutu was the greatest thrill of her life. It sounded like a final statement of some kind." Faith affirmed that she had refused to let her get help. She even seemed upset when she learned that I was a doctor. I assured them that I was available at a moment's notice.

About four in the morning I was awakened by Faith, who asked me to come quickly. She believed that Mrs. Porter was dead. Nan and I went to her room. The minute I saw her, it was obvious that she was gone. I examined her. Her heart was stopped and her skin was ice cold. There was no point in CPR (cardiopulmonary resuscitation). We tidied her up and made her as presentable as possible. Now what to do? I cautioned everyone that no word of this must reach the rest of the camp, especially the staff, until we had made a plan as to how the situation should be handled. Faith managed to get us all some hot tea from the awakening kitchen staff for it was now about five in the morning. The camp was alive and preparing for another day. Miss Campbell, Mrs. Porter's traveling companion, my wife Nan and I sat discussing the options available to us while we sipped our tea and watched the dawn break over the horizon of the Serengeti.

I knew that we must make every effort to get her body to Kenya. If she were reported dead in Tanzania, it was entirely possible that the authorities would insist that the body be moved to Dar es Salaam for an autopsy, probably by surface transport and without refrigeration. I doubted that refrigeration would be available at the coroner in Dar es Salaam either. Endless forms would be required. I thought that David and Faith would probably be required to accompany her, which would hold them up for several days at least. There was no US Ambassador at Dar es Salaam, only a consul who might be less effective in expediting the red tape than the Ambassador in Kenya. It was obvious that the best course of action would be to get the body to Kenya any way we could.

Given the state of relations between Kenya and Tanzania that existed at that time, cooperation in transferring a dead American tourist across the border was likely to be exceedingly difficult at best. It was a problem that none of us was eager to face. Certainly no one wanted the responsibility. I knew that the Flying Doctors were not permitted to transport bodies across any border in East Africa without proper government authorization; a complicated process. That she was a tourist and a foreign national promised only to make matters even more difficult. It could be political dynamite if we were caught transporting her body surreptitiously. As a founder and director of the Flying Doctors I hated to break the rules, however, to go by the book promised to be incredibly inconvenient.

I thought about all possible options—smuggling her by car at night, hiding her body in the trunk hoping to fool the border guards, and so forth. Evacuating her by air to Kenya was the only practical solution. At that time the Flying Doctors had clearance to fly across the Tanzania-Kenya border at any time without the necessity of clearing customs and immigration. It was up to me to somehow get a plane out to the Ndutu strip. I needed to persuade Flying Doctors headquarters to dispatch a plane, and then after the plane arrived, to convince the pilot and nurse to take her to Nairobi. Again, I admonished everyone in our little group not to reveal to anyone in the camp that Mrs. Porter had died. News travels very fast in Africa.

Tor Allan's Range Rover had a single-side-band short wave radio equipped with the special frequency assigned to the Flying Doctors. While the others ate breakfast, I raised Flying Doctors headquarters at Wilson Airport. Kirsten Benneke, a Danish nurse on duty in the radio room answered my call. She was new with the Flying Doctors, having been hired only the week before. The transmission was clear on the frequency, as yet uncluttered by chattering voices. "Good morning AMREF [the proper name for the Flying Doctors]," I said. "This is Dr. Thomas Rees calling from Ndutu in Tanzania. I have a patient with a very serious problem here." "Good morning doctor," said Kirsten "Please state your problem."

Things were not starting as I had hoped. I had not met Nurse Kirsten yet. I was not sure that she knew who I was and where I stood in the organization. "There is an American woman tourist here who is very sick. I need to evacuate her to Nairobi as quickly as possible. How soon can you get a plane?" Following her instructions to the letter according to the manual, she replied, "Please tell me her symptoms and describe her examination before I locate the duty pilot."

"Please, you don't understand," I insisted. "This woman is critically ill. I cannot give her adequate treatment here. I am afraid she will die if we do not get her to hospital."

"Please tell me what her pulse, temperature, and blood pressure are." she dutifully asked. "Nurse," I said, "this patient is in a very bad way. Please trust my judgement. Who is the duty pilot this morning? Please let me talk with him. I do not have much time."

"The pilot is Phil Mathews," she said, "but doctor, we really must have more information before we can send a plane." My frustration level was rising rapidly. I turned to Tor Allan who was sitting next to me and was grimly amused at my problem. Tor commented that I was undoubtedly speaking to a new nurse who was following the manual scrupulously. He thought that she was probably nervous about making the decision herself. "Nurse, please do as I say. Call Phil Mathews and tell him that Dr. Tom Rees is on the radio, and that I urgently need a plane at Ndutu. I will stand by while you make the call." I put on my most authoritative voice. "Yes Doctor," she said with a note of uncertainty (or was it resentment) in her voice.

A few minutes later, which seemed an eternity, she was back on the frequency. She said that Mathews had okayed the flight. I could expect the plane in about an hour-and-a-half, perhaps slightly longer since there was still some early morning ground fog at Wilson. Now all I had to do was to convince our pilot, Phil Mathews to go along with the plan. I knew it would be a tough decision for him. Could I get him to risk his license? Tanzania would certainly go hard on him, even if Kenya didn't.

Tor Allan and I chewed over our options. What would be the safest and most expeditious way of transporting Mrs. Porter's body to Nairobi without getting anyone in trouble? Fortuitously, Tor remembered that he had met the officer in charge of police at Arusha, the nearest town of any size in Tanzania, and certainly the regional governing authority for Ndutu. We decided to tackle the problem head on and to radio the police station in Arusha and request clearance for moving the body to Kenya.

Tor managed to contact police headquarters at Arusha and, to our good fortune, talk with the officer in charge whom he knew. After explaining our predicament Tor turned the radio over to me to convince the man that Mrs. Porter had died of natural causes and there was no suspicion whatsoever of foul play. The conversation was long and difficult, but at last to my intense relief, the police officer approved of our moving Mrs. Porter's remains to Nairobi by direct flight, provided I would promise, without fail, to obtain and send him a proper legal affidavit attesting to our lady's death by natural causes in lieu of a Tanzanian death certificate. I fulfilled my promise immediately after I returned to Nairobi.

Now my problem was how to get the body from her room to the airstrip without being detected by the staff who, I was sure, would be greatly upset to learn that one of their guests had died. The manager of the camp was an Indian, Mr. Gupta, who, I was sure, would not wish to get involved in any way for fear of running afoul of the authorities. In consultation with the Joneses and Nan, we decided to wrap her body in a blanket, back the Land Rover up to her door, move her into the back of the car, and whisk her off to the strip.

To my amusement, the three men in my safari party refused to have anything to do with this maneuver. I needed help to wrap her up and move her. Our fearless guide, Tor Allan, big game hunter and bush expert and six foot-two David Niven, as well as Donald McPherson, would have no part in the move. Nothing would persuade them to touch the body or help me carry it. Finally, I relied on the "weaker sex" to help. Nan, Faith Jones and I wrapped her in a blanket. Huffing and puffing, we lugged her into the back of the Land Rover although she was longer than the back of the car and her feet hung beyond the rear edge. Nan and Faith got in back to hold her in as we bounced along the rutted track to the airstrip. The entrance to the kitchen was on our route past the service buildings. Many curious faces watched our progress as we drove through the camp.

The Cessna landed in a cloud of dust and rolled to a stop. I drove up to the side door. Out stepped Phil Mathews and Nurse Kirsten. They both took one look at our bundle and realized what we were up to. "No way am I going to fly a body back to Nairobi, Tom, you know it's against the law. I could get my butt in a big jam for this. I could even lose my pilot's license." I assured him that all was well. I told him I had obtained permission from the police at Arusha for the transport and I would take full responsibility with the Kenyan authorities, although I anticipated no difficulty. I suggested that all he had to do was take off and when he crossed the border, radio headquarters that he was bringing in a DOA (dead on arrival) case. I promised that I would contact the AMREF doctor on duty by radio and have him standing by with an ambulance on their arrival. The doctor could pronounce her a DOA. The American Embassy would then take over. End of story.

Nurse Kirsten had a special concern of her own. She was on one of her first emergency flights for the Flying Doctors. She knew who I was by now, but this did little to relieve her anxiety. "Dr. Rees, it will reflect badly on my professional reputation to bring in a deceased patient having just started with the Flying Docs. It would be embarrassing to say the least."

I pointed out yet again that we had permission from the Tanzanian authorities and went on to explain what dealing with the body in Tanzania would entail. I appealed to her sense of responsibility to the deceased's family and to all of us.

My persuasion did the job. We loaded the body onto the airplane stretcher. The plane took off and headed towards Kenya. We all sighed with relief. I radioed the Flying Doctors from Tor's car and managed to get the duty doctor of the day. Using parables, I managed to convey what we were up to. Not amused, but detecting the note of desperation in my voice, and recognizing that the plan was already under way and sanctioned by the Tanzanian police, he promised to cooperate.

The plane landed and taxied to the Flying Doctors' hangar where it was met by an ambulance. All went smoothly and without interference by officialdom. The doctor on duty pronounced her dead on arrival. The official report noted that she had died of cardiac failure. The staff at the American Embassy were most helpful in expediting all arrangements. The explanation of the events surrounding her death was never questioned. She was cremated in Nairobi according to her prearranged instructions. Her ashes were spread over the Mara in Kenya in final union with her beloved husband.

Several days later, enjoying a drink on the veranda at the Norfolk Hotel in Nairobi, Faith Jones told me that Mrs. Porter had asked her several times what the name "Ndutu" meant. No one knew. Sometime later, I met a Maasai in the Mara who had grown up near Ndutu. He said that Ndutu is a Maasai word that means "a place of peace."

When I returned to America, I wrote to Mrs. Porter's son. I told the story of our encounter during her last twenty-four hours on this earth. I told him how she had fulfilled the final dream shared by her husband and herself—she had seen the Ngorongoro Crater and the great migration in the Serengeti. I described how she had died in her sleep, been moved to Nairobi for cremation and had finally been joined with her husband on the plains of Africa. I told him that she had died in Ndutu, "a place of peace," appropriately named as a final destination of her fulfilled dream.

AMREF RADIO AND FLYING COMMUNICATIONS NETWORK

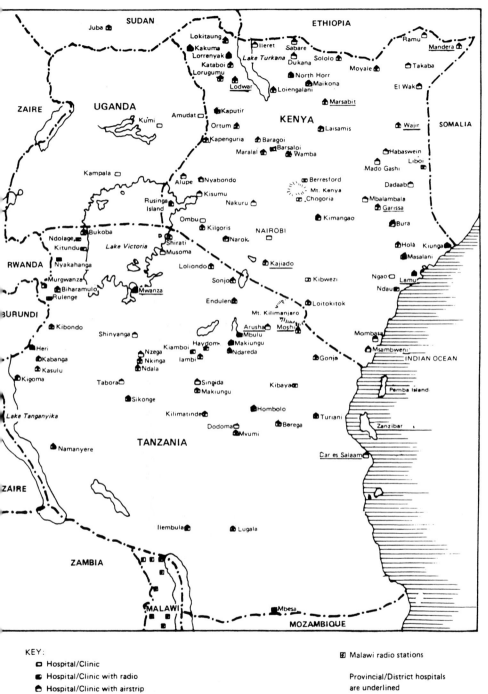

KEY:
- ▢ Hospital/Clinic
- ▪ Hospital/Clinic with radio
- ◗ Hospital/Clinic with airstrip

▣ Malawi radio stations

Provincial/District hospitals
are underlined

A map in the Radio Room of the Flying Doctors detailing the locations of
the Radio Communications Network, bush hospitals, clinics, and landing strips.

Sir Archibald McIndoe,
one of the three founders of AMREF and The Flying Doctors.

The author with Sir Michael Wood (left), co-founder of The Flying Doctors.
Michael was the spearhead and Director General of AMREF for many years.

Sir Michael and Lady Susan Wood

The author flanked by Leonora Semler on his right who has worked tirelessly on behalf of AMREF and The Flying Doctors for more than 35 years as head of the German branch of AMREF. On the author's left is Dr. Anne Spoerry, the famous "Mama Daktari."

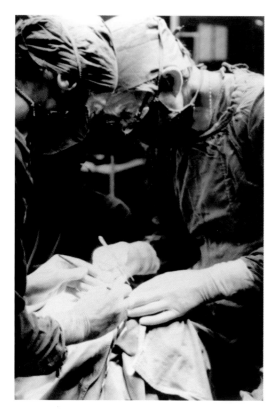

The author operating at the Christian Medical Center at Moshi, Tanzania (1985).

Our first airplane, the Piper Tripacer lands on the soccer field at Shirati, Tanzania (1962). We were immediately surrounded by curious "watu" (people).

Nan Rees and Michael Wood surrounded by villagers at Shirati.

The author prepares for a surgical outreach mission to Tanzania with a surgical team and pilots. Maggie Maina (far left of photo) is the chief nurse of clinical surgery. On her left is Dr. John Wachira, staff surgeon for AMREF.

The Flying Doctors air fleet at our hanger in Nairobi, Kenya.

The pride of the fleet, a Cessna Grand Caravan. The plane can carry four stretchers and a full load of EMS equipment and personnel.

Stuck in the mud, a not uncommon sight during the rainy season.
Michael Wood is pushing the nose of the plane.

The author and Sir Michael Wood together on a surgical safari (1982).

A child with a cleft lip and severe malnutrition. In rural Africa, children with deformities often have multiple other health problems as well.

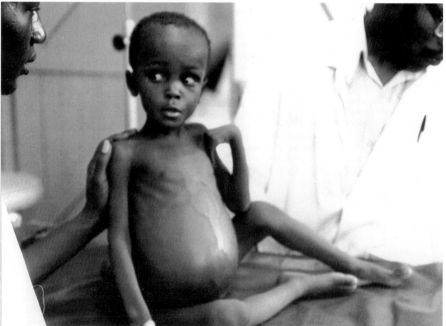

A child with the typical swollen belly and chocolate colored skin of protein deficiency so common in areas of drought or war.

Severe burn scarring in a young boy, a common problem in rural Africa where children are prone to fall into open cooking fires.

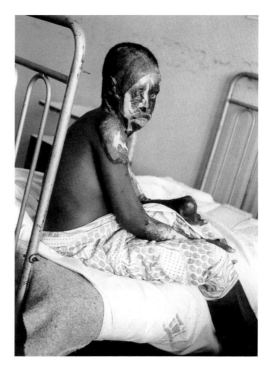

A young boy with Burkitt's tumor of the neck at Shirati, Tanzania (1962). This cancer is one of the first identified to be of viral origin.

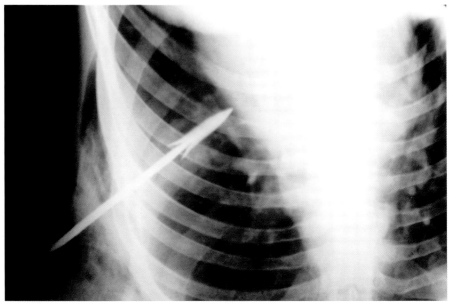

An arrow shot by a jealous husband that pierced the chest wall and entered the stomach of a man suspected of cheating with his wife at Kaimosi (1962).

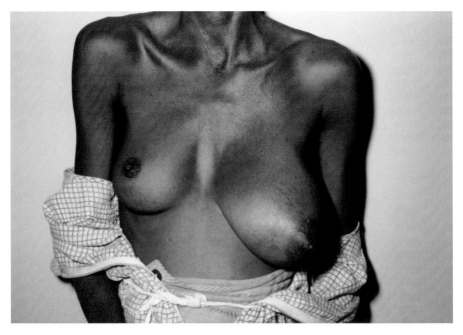

The favorite wife of a tribal chief who was in danger of losing her favored position because of her breast asymmetry. Successfully treated by reducing the large breast (mammaplasty) to match the smaller one in Tanzania (1962).

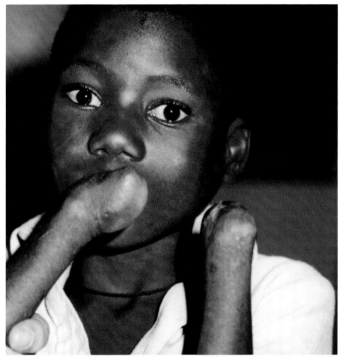

A boy who lost both hands at the wrist from a hyena attack
as he protected his father's goat herd.

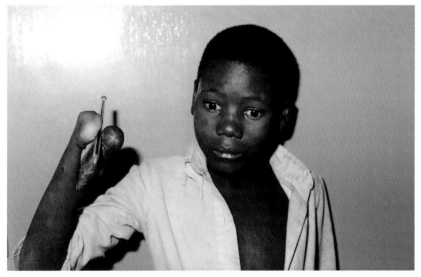

At operation, a "lobster claw" was constructed to enable him to dress himself and
even write. Operation by Dr. Bill Adams-Ray and the author at the Christian
Medical Center, Moshi, Tanzania (1988).

Immunizations at a bush clinic in Maasailand by nurse
Winnifred Robinson ("Robbie"), 1972.

The author with the famous "Mama Daktari," Dr. Anne Spoerry who flew her
own plane, attending to clinics in remote areas for over 35 years with The Flying
Doctors. Anne was much loved by her African patients and by the entire staff.
She flew her clinic rounds until her death at the age of 80 in 1999.

The Staff of AMREF at The Flying Doctor's hanger (1994).

An AMREF nurse comforts two Turkana boys at Lodwar (1990).

The author's wife, Nan in 2001, a tireless fundraiser for The Flying Doctors.

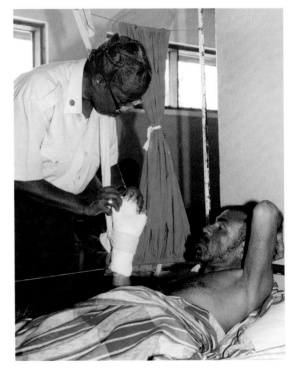

Dr. Marlene Long, a staff plastic surgeon for The Flying Doctors examines the result of her operation for reconstruction of the hand of a leprosy patient.

The author with Nicky Blundell-Brown, an indispensable coordinator of AMREF
and Flying Doctor activities for over 30 years.

The author (right) with Jim Heather-Hayes who has been a pilot for over 35 years
with The Flying Doctors and is currently Chief of Aviation. Circa 1978.

Lady Sue Wood in 2002. Much loved by everyone in AMREF.

Three key figures in the development of the Outreach Surgical Program
of The Flying Doctors (left to right):
Dr. Tom Raassen, a Dutch general surgeon, chief of surgery for AMREF and
coordinator of the Surgical Outreach Program;
Dr. John Wachira, a Kenya general surgeon with special training in urology,
team leader, and full-time surgeon for AMREF; and
Dr. Bill Adams-Ray, a Swedish reconstructive surgeon who served 12 years
as a staff surgeon for AMREF, and was responsible for the leprosy and
reconstructive surgery program, and is now an academic surgeon in Sweden.

10

Uganda Adventure

During the night of January 27, 1971, one of the twentieth century's supreme monsters, General Idi Amin "Dada" mounted a military coup in Uganda that overthrew the government of President Apollo Milton Obote, not exactly a benign despot himself, while Obote was attending a Commonwealth heads of government conference in Singapore. At first light the next day, three of us, shivering in the chill of the Nairobi dawn, loaded our surgical equipment and personal kit into 5Y-AFD, a Cessna 206 turbo-charged, single-engine aircraft belonging to the Flying Doctors.

Landing on short, dirt airstrips is dangerous and tricky, especially at the high altitudes sometimes encountered in East Africa. To make our trips as safe as possible, we'd had our plane's wings modified with a Robertson stall kit. The modification allowed the plane to fly more slowly for landings, and get into the air more quickly on take-offs. Planes modified like ours are the workhorses of bush flying, everywhere. High-wing Cessnas, even without the modification, are desirable because their wingtips can clear the grass or bush that frequently crowd the boundaries of unimproved landing strips.

The control tower gradually emerged through the morning mist as we wheeled the plane out of the hangar. Sweaters were worn to ward off the morning chill, but they would be shed when we flew into the heat of the northern Uganda desert. At almost a mile high, Nairobi cools off during the night, despite its proximity to the equator. We hustled along, eager to be the first plane out that morning.

Seroti in northern Uganda was our destination and it would be a long flight. The dirt strip at Seroti was the closest to our final destination. An intensive two days of surgery was scheduled at the leprosy hospital at Kumi. Our surgical safari was one of a regularly scheduled series of visits by our plastic surgery team, who provided the only expertise available in this vast area capable of repairing the ravages of leprosy.

I was in Africa at the time on one of my yearly working visits. The other surgeon on the team was Dr. Richard Kostecki of Watertown, Connecticut, who was spending a year in Africa with the Flying Doctors as a special CARE-MEDICO Fellow in reconstructive surgery. Our pilot, Dave Allen, a veteran with hundreds of hours in the air and extensive experience as a bush pilot, was there to see that we made the trip safely. Dave knew every square mile of East Africa, and was well acquainted with almost all of the bush strips. He had flown extensively in the Congo during the revolution.

The plane was carefully pre-flighted. A forced landing in the hostile environment of the desert is not an adventure welcomed by anyone. Flying around Africa with Mike Wood for a few years had stimulated me to learn to fly myself, if for no other reason than self-preservation. I wanted to be capable of landing the plane safely should something happen to the pilot. Flying over the vast areas of the East African bush, there is always the thought lurking in the back of one's mind that an emergency landing is a possibility. Eventually I took flying lessons, planning to become proficient enough just to land a plane in an emergency. Predictably, I became hooked on flying. Many hours and several thousands of dollars later, I ended up a qualified pilot with an instrument rating.

Cessna 5Y-AFD warmed up without a glitch. A large red cross adorned the tail and "EAST AFRICAN FLYING DOCTOR SERVICES" on the fuselage identified the aircraft. "Do you want to fly her this morning Tom?" asked Dave. "Sure," I said, thrilled at the opportunity. It would be my first time at the controls on a bona fide Flying Doctors' flight. I had been looking forward to this day for a long time, a goal that I had secretly nurtured for years. "Take over then, but don't forget, Nairobi is getting on for six thousand feet in the air, and you must lean out the fuel mixture during your take-off roll. And remember to stand on the brakes until you get the power full on before you release."

I taxied to the holding area on runway zero-seven and ran up the engine. With everything OK we were given clearance for take-off. I stood on the brakes while advancing the throttle to full take-off power. The plane shuddered and vibrated, pulling against the brakes. There was no wind, so no correction of the controls was necessary. I released the brakes and, unrestrained, the Cessna leapt forward and gathered speed down the runway. I leaned the carburetor mixture control, mindful of Dave's instructions. We gathered speed through the tendrils of mist that still remained, and at last were off. As soon as we were airborne the tower instructed me to make a right turn over the Nairobi National Park, and come around to a northwesterly heading for Uganda.

We carried all of the instruments and surgical paraphernalia that we would need for the journey. With the weight of the equipment, ourselves and our overnight kits, plus full fuel tanks, the plane was at its maximum gross weight. We climbed slowly through the thin cool air of the Nairobi plateau.

"Good morning Entebbe," I radioed—the usual greeting to identify ourselves and confirm our flight plan with Uganda as we crossed the Kenya-Uganda border. "This is Five-Yankee Alpha-Foxtrot-Delta Flying Doctors en route Nairobi to Seroti. Request permission to proceed direct Seroti." "Five-Yankee Alpha-Foxtrot-Delta this is Uganda control. You are instructed to change course and fly directly to Entebbe International Airport where you are to land and await further instructions."

We were totally surprised at this response. "Entebbe, Entebbe." Dave had taken the mike and was speaking now, "We are a Flying Doctor's aircraft on a routine medical flight to Seroti. We filed with East Africa Control this morning. Again request permission to fly Seroti direct. Do you read?"

"Negative Five-Yankee Alpha-Foxtrot-Delta. Do as you are instructed. Fly direct Entebbe and land. Failure to comply will result in our intercepting you with a fighter plane." We all wondered what the hell this could be all about, and came to the same conclusion: We had better do what they say. They just might get rough with us. We certainly didn't want to fool around with a fighter. Discretion being the better part of valor, we flew to Entebbe.

On final approach to the runway at Entebbe I could see that the airport was in a state of chaos. Land Rovers, trucks, half-tracks and other vehicles, most in camouflage paint, were everywhere. Men were scattered about singly and in groups. Machine guns were set up behind sandbags at strategic locations. Anti-tank and anti-aircraft guns were mounted on many of the vehicles. As we came to a full stop at the refueling tanks, more details were visible. There was no uniform dress code among these troops. Some wore khakis with military insignia, while others were in camouflage uniforms. Quite a few men were in blue jeans with military style shirts and berets. Dark glasses were worn by many. Combat boots, sandals and sports shoes comprised the footwear.

Uzi machine pistols and rifles dangled by sling straps nonchalantly, while grenades and ammunition pouches hung from many jackets. It looked like a scene out of the movies, except these players were very real indeed.

A battered DC-3 in camouflage paint was refueling, while several single-engine airplanes were scattered in disarray about the airport. Commercial airliners were conspicuous by their absence in this usually busy international airport. To our frustration, no fighter planes were seen. We speculated that their threats had been hollow. The controller ordered us to taxi immediately to the general passenger terminal. As the propeller wound down, we were instantly surrounded by young men who pointed automatic weapons at us. Certainly there was no evidence of military organization amongst our captors, who were aimlessly milling about, except for two or three who kept us under guard, weapons at the ready.

I searched in vain for some insignia or identifying characteristics of a leader. Our attempts to strike up a conversation failed. Our questions were met with silence. One man with an Uzi finally pointed to the door of the terminal. *Pesi pesi* (hurry) he said. We filed into the waiting room of the general terminal, prodded at each step by gun muzzles in our backs. The waiting room was empty except for ourselves, our guards and a wire-spectacled Indian clerk behind the counter. Obviously nervous, the clerk declined to answer any questions.

After what seemed an eternity, a young African in his twenties strutted into the room. Judging from the respect shown by our guards, he was their leader. He was quite handsome, dressed in a camouflage jacket and trousers with captain's "pips" on his shoulders, a paratrooper-type beret, highly polished paratrooper boots and the ubiquitous dark glasses. An Uzi hung from his shoulder and a Browning high-power nine-millimenter pistol hung on his belt. I questioned him, but he ignored me. English was taught as a primary language in most schools in Uganda, as well as Swahili, so that I was quite sure he understood me.

"Maybe he really doesn't understand English; why don't you talk to him in Swahili?" I asked Dave. My Swahili was limited to a few words and phrases. Dave got the same stonewalling that I had. Since we could get no response, I again decided to pump the Indian clerk who was obviously unnerved by it all. The only news forthcoming from him was that there had been a coup the night before and the government had been overthrown by someone named Amin. He also said that officials at the airport were either in jail or had been executed. That was all he knew.

My irritation level was growing by the minute. I tried again and again to get some kind of response out of our captors, only to be met with stony stares and continued silence. In my naivete, I believed that a United States Passport was respected anywhere in the world and probably would intimidate our captors. Approaching desperation, Dr. Kostecki and I produced our passports declaring that we were US Citizens and demanded to speak to whomever was in charge of the airport, as well as the US Consul. Again, our efforts were to no avail. The impotent situation we found ourselves in began to take its toll on my patience. In fact, the whole thing pissed me off. No one seemed capable of making a decision about us. I wondered if we were casualties of the confusion. It seemed we were under house arrest at the airport until someone decided what to do with us.

We sat waiting for several hours, increasingly annoyed that we were losing the better part of the day, which had been fully scheduled for surgery at the Kumi leprosy center, still many miles to the north. It finally began to dawn on me (through my anger) that perhaps we were truly in danger, not just being inconvenienced. In the meantime, we could see through the window that the plane was being stripped of its seats and all of our equipment and personal effects were strewn on the ground.

The "leader" eventually left us alone with two armed guards. He returned after about an hour and explained in excellent English that we were being detained, as were all foreigners in Uganda, following the military coup of their "liberator," General Idi Amin. If and when it was determined by higher authority than he that we were not spies, we would be released.

I guess my reaction was typically American and naive. I was incensed at this invasion of my freedom. I still believed that US passports would work magic in foreign countries, and chagrined that mine did not. The disregard for our medical and surgical supplies astounded me. I assumed that even uneducated soldiers would respect medical equipment. Dave, who held a British passport, was not so amazed at this lack of reverence. His experience with mercenaries and revolutionary soldiers in the Congo had left him with no illusions about the power of documents. He did have plenty of respect, however, for the potentially dangerous situation we were in. He wisely remained silent during our indignant outbursts.

At one point, Dave whispered to me "For God's sake be careful. You don't understand the mentality of these young revolutionaries. Remember that most of them are probably not trained professional soldiers. They're flushed with victory and running on adrenaline. They couldn't care less about you or your citizenship. They'll shoot if we give them a problem. Just swallow your pride and go along with it. I've seen this all before in the Congo. Don't push your luck." Dave's warning made sense to me. I realized I was behaving rather stupidly. An American passport meant nothing to this man, nor did the fact that we belonged to an international medical organization.

After stripping the plane of everything movable and thoroughly searching us and our equipment, and finding nothing to indicate that we were spies or otherwise dangerous characters, his suspicious attitude waned. Finally, with some obvious indecision, he consented to let us continue on our flight in a short while. I believe that he had received instructions from someone of higher authority. Possibly our insistence that they put us in contact with the US Consul had finally made them nervous.

During the early hours of our detainment, the demeanor of the leader was aggressive, arrogant and at times menacing, but as the day progressed his attitude mellowed. I now attribute his arrogance to his insecurity and youth, along with the excitement of being part of a victorious military coup. He was filled with a sense of power and excitement, all of which colored his attitude toward us. I doubt he knew a great deal more than we did about the details of the coup.

As I felt more comfortable with him, I asked to be put in touch with the Minister of Health or the supervisor of the airport. I explained who the Flying Doctors were and what we did for his fellow Ugandans. I was sure that the authorities would clear up this dilemma since they both knew of the work of the Flying Doctors. He admitted that because both were enemies of the new government, they had been killed during the capture of the airport.

Late in the afternoon, he told us to pack the airplane, that we were free to go and cleared to Seroti. Re-packing our gear and the airplane took over an hour. We were truly annoyed that we had lost an entire operating day. Our tight schedule made the hours precious. We had only allowed two days to get through all of the surgical cases awaiting us; we would have to work practically all night to catch up.

As we were packing the plane I asked the leader for permission to fly directly back to Nairobi from Seroti after finishing our surgical schedule the next day. I explained that because of our detention we would now have to work overtime to complete our surgical schedule, and therefore we would be flying back to Kenya late in the day. We needed to arrive in Nairobi before dark, because there were no landing lights at Wilson Airport. Returning through Entebbe would require us to cancel several operations in order to leave the hospital early. I hoped that logic might appeal to his better nature. I reminded him that the plane as well as ourselves had been searched and that there would be nothing new to find the next day. "I will try to get clearance for you to return to Nairobi direct tomorrow," he said, "but I cannot promise anything. It will depend on what my commanding officer decides."

Finally, we took off and headed north. Late in the afternoon we sighted the dirt strip at Seroti. As we rolled to a stop at the end of the runway, two men armed with rifles beckoned us to get out of the plane. They were policemen from their post at Seroti. They knew from listening to the radio that a coup had taken place, but knew nothing of the details. The particulars of the revolution had not yet reached the hinterlands. These policemen knew our aircraft very well since it had made many trips to Seroti; nevertheless they were nervous, not knowing the details of the events of the preceding twenty-four hours. Without direction, they were unsure how to deal with us.

To play it safe, we were promptly thrown into the one-room local jail, probably while they waited for orders. We were contemplating a night of misery in this small cell with no furniture, beds or plumbing facilities, except for a hole in the middle of the floor from which a terrible stench arose. To our great relief, about an hour later a young Dutch doctor from the leprosarium rescued us. He was known to the police and confirmed that we were an expected surgical team to work at Kumi. He signed for our release.

On the way to the hospital we recounted our adventures of the long, trying day. "We thought the coup might delay you," he said. "We have heard bits and pieces of it over the radio, but we have no clear news except that this fellow Amin seems to be in control of the country."

The road to Kumi was appalling, even by East African standards. It had rained the previous two days and the road was slick as grease, pot-holed and muddy. The vintage Land Rover slithered along the ruts sounding like it was on its last legs. We were starving, having had no food all day except for a cup of tea. At the hospital a prodigious Dutch dinner was produced with beautiful fresh vegetables, a stew and fruit for desert. We were told by a proud staff that the resident patients in the leper colony grew the vegetables and fruit. After dinner we examined the patients scheduled for surgery. It was tough breaking the news that there was no way we could complete the entire list of operations as scheduled, we were simply out of time.

We were going to operate under difficult conditions. Water for the operating rooms had to be carried in by hand from a well, since there was no running water available. There was also no generator so that we had to jury rig lights from one of the Land Rovers. It was clear that we would have to operate far into the night to try to catch up. Despite these inconveniences the staff were cheerful and did everything possible to make us comfortable. We worked through the night until early in the morning, then refueled with strong Dutch coffee and hot bread. The work was fascinating and we forgot our fatigue. We grabbed three hours of sleep and resumed our schedule.

As so often happens on a surgical safari, it was impossible to complete the scheduled list of patients. We were committed to arrive in Nairobi before dark. Reluctantly, we also had to plan on a stop at Entebbe again on our way to Kenya unless we could get radio clearance to go direct. That afternoon, we thanked our gracious

Dutch hosts and jostled back to the airstrip at Seroti. What had been mud the day before had now dried into a nightmare of ruts, bumps, and grooves. I prayed that I would not rupture a disk on the way. We pre-flighted the airplane, filled it with fuel and took off with just enough time to make it back before dark, factoring in an hour's detour to Entebbe.

After an hour, the Kenya border was growing nearer. Dave and I discussed taking a calculated risk and making a run for it—to hell with Entebbe. I was all for it, but Dave's cool head prevailed. He pointed out that such an action might jeopardize all future Flying Doctors' flights into Uganda. "Good afternoon Entebbe, this is Flying Doctors Cessna Five-Yankee Alpha-Foxtrot-Delta on a scheduled flight from Seroti, requesting routing direct to Nairobi," said Dave. "That is a negative Five-Yankee Alpha-Foxtrot-Delta. You are to proceed immediately to Entebbe and land."

"Please check with airport command for possible instructions regarding us," Dave said, "We were inspected yesterday at Entebbe en route to Seroti. We requested permission then to fly direct to Kenya today." "Proceed directly to Entebbe at this time and land." snapped the controller. He didn't need to remind us about the fighter plane threat of yesterday.

Once more we debated making a low-level dash for the Kenya border, but agreed—all factors considered—it was not the wise thing to do. We landed and taxied to the terminal, where the performance of the first day was repeated. The airplane was again stripped. Our personal gear, surgical equipment and instruments were strewn on the ground. We were led into the terminal building where each of us was subjected to a personal body search. My camera, used to document operations, was snatched out of my hand, the film removed, and ignoring my entreaties to save it, exposed and ruined. I was enraged by this demeaning act.

I was once again on the edge of losing it when Dave brought me abruptly back to reality. "Don't do anything stupid, Tom. I promise you these guys can be unpredictable. They don't give a damn about you, the Flying Doctors or anything else just now. Just grin and bear it and for God's sake don't put us all in danger with a temper tantrum. There just is no one to appeal to here." Of course, I knew that he was right. Clenching my teeth, I concentrated on being as civil and cooperative as I could. I just wanted to get the hell out of there and get back to Nairobi. To my disappointment, the leader of the group that had detained us the previous day was no where in evidence. I had hoped that he would promptly clear us.

The contents of the plane were being roughly searched. Two men with army boots were trampling on our surgical instruments, destroying many of them. This trashing of our equipment seemed designed to humiliate us rather than have any meaningful purpose. We grimly kept our silence. There was really nothing that we could do to stop them. Finally, we were saved from further abuse by an African man who appeared to be about forty years old, wearing a British-type field uniform with major's insignias on his epaulets. He was evidently in command. He was not pleased with the actions of the younger soldiers who were having fun at our expense.

Apologizing for the behavior of the troops, he introduced himself. He knew of the Flying Doctors. He praised our work in Uganda and added that he hoped we would not stop our activities because of the change of government. He assured us that Amin would do great things for Uganda. "All of the Army is behind him," he said. "Obote's government could no longer be tolerated. Now we will have justice and prosperity for all." Familiar words after a revolution. At his command, the equipment and our personal gear were returned to their proper places in the plane. He ordered that we be refueled. "You can proceed back to Nairobi. Be sure and tell everyone that we here in Uganda are very happy with the change and that General Amin will not only be good for Uganda but for all of East Africa as well."

Wasting little time, we got airborne as quickly as possible and set our course for the Kenya border. The last light was beginning to fade as we squeaked into Wilson airport; the last plane to do so that day. After securing the plane and unloading our damaged equipment we went straight to the Dambusters Bar and downed a refreshing glass of beer. I learned more about the revolution from friends that night at dinner. Resistance by troops loyal to Obote's government had been sporadic and brief. All opposition was brutally dealt with by Amin, establishing a pattern that would become the hallmark of his tenure as chief of state in Uganda. Officers who resisted him were summarily executed. Those who escaped execution fled the country by whatever means they could.

Amin's rule of Uganda was a showcase of terror and horror of our time. Hundreds of thousands were tortured and slaughtered by this despot. Uganda was destroyed as a country, stripped of human, agricultural and animal resources. Schools, universities and hospitals were closed, and all social services became extinct. During the Ugandan revolution, the Flying Doctors were forced to cancel all their activities in the country. Our equipment, including eight radios located in rural hospitals, was confiscated by Amin. We watched helplessly the near total destruction of the country's health system, including the prestigious medical school in Kampala, by his regime.

Today, after Amin's ouster, Uganda is busy rebuilding itself. The Flying Doctors have been warmly welcomed back and are actively involved once more in many health projects there.

11

Samburu Maiden

The tire exploded with a loud bang and the car, overloaded and top heavy, began to fishtail down the road. It swerved sickeningly from side to side. Deep borrow pits lined both sides of the gravel road. If I lost control, the safari car could easily roll over the side, with catastrophic consequences. The car was without windows or safety belts, which concerned me, as my elderly father sat in the back, next to the door. If we rolled, he would surely fall out.

Don't step on the brakes; let the car run its course; just lift off the accelerator; turn into it; don't overcorrect! I repeated the rules of off-road driving in my head over and over, like a mantra. After what seemed an eternity, we came to a stop. The sun blazed down. It was at least 100 degrees F.

The car belonged to Monty Ruben, a long-time fixture in Nairobi. A third generation African of European descent, the film business was Monte's specialty. Movie companies shooting in Kenya found him to be an invaluable source of local knowledge. Monty knew every inch of the back country intimately. He also knew everyone who counted both in and out of government—who to see and how to get things done. Monty had elected for Kenyan citizenship when Uhuru (independence) came. Citizenship had been offered to all Kenyans of all races by President Kenyatta. The car I was driving had recently been custom-built by a body shop in Nairobi specializing in adapting vehicles for the safari trade. It had begun its life as a Toyota Land Cruiser. The safari car was his pride and joy, sturdy and rugged. Unfortunately, it was also top heavy when loaded and unstable when a blowout occurred, which was frequently on roads like this. Replacing the blown tire, which was in shreds, proved a sweaty and difficult job. After much pulling, pushing and swearing, the tire was changed and we were on our way again, driving north to Marsabit.

The only road from Nairobi to Ethiopia runs north from Archer's Post near the Samburu Game Reserve. It is maintained by the government at irregular intervals, depending on available funds. Civilian travel on this road can be dangerous, due to ongoing unrest and frequent civil wars in neighboring countries. Armed gangs of bandits, poachers and exiled soldiers from Ethiopia, Somalia and Sudan often rove the area, seeking victims. Well adapted to life in the desert, such bandit gangs lent an air of uncertainty to every trip through the region. Nowadays, armed guards accompany automobiles traveling along the Marsabit Road in convoys. We were traveling alone.

A formidable desert blankets the northern frontier of Kenya. Nomads, accustomed to hardship, inhabit this vast area, herding and scratching a meager living from the hostile environment. North of Archer's Post are the granite cliffs of Ololokwe, frosted white from vulture droppings. The mountains are reminiscent of *King Solomon's Mines*, rising at intervals from the otherwise flat landscape. Between mountain ranges, the desert stretches in all directions as far as the eye can see. Like the surface of the moon, the land is desolate but hauntingly beautiful. One of the largest freshwater lakes in the world, Lake Turkana, occupies a huge area in the midst of this bone-dry landscape; yet elsewhere, water is scarce, completely absent during droughts. The nomads constantly move their livestock, following the water supply and marginal vegetation that sprouts after rain. When the rains come, water is found in ancient wells and seasonal rivers.

When the rains are sparse, the wells dry up, river beds turn into sand and every scraggly piece of vegetation dies. Drought, more severe some years than others, follows a cycle of several years' duration. When it rains the desert blooms and the grass grows green. In good times, the cattle and goats grow fat and the people prosper. When the rains fail, as they frequently do, it is catastrophic for both animals and people.

Lake Paradise, in an extinct volcanic crater in the mountains of Marsabit, was our destination. We traveled fast to keep the car on top of the washboard surface and to avoid shaking it (and us) to pieces. A dense cloud of swirling dust trailed us for half a mile or more. Bandannas filtered some of the dust from our mouths and lungs. We looked like bandits from some western movie or visitors from another planet—the dust people. We were covered with fine white powder from head to toe. Showing through our dusty bandannas were the moist outlines of our mouths and noses, and above, our parched, red-rimmed eyes. Every crevice of the car, our duffels, camera bags, camping equipment and food boxes was penetrated by the dust.

The so-called "long" rains of the previous year, due in April and May, had been scanty. The "short" rains that had been due in October and November failed altogether. It was now February and it had not rained for many months. All moisture had long since sought refuge deep in the desert sand. Water holes and wells, which once provided sustenance for camels, goats, cattle and humans, were now only shallow craters lined with hard-dried mud, reticulated with deep cracks. The bleached white bones of goats and cattle now littered the roadside. Filtered through the dust, the light assumed an eerie orange-red tint, making the carcasses look like modern, surrealistic sculptures.

What few animals we passed were in desperate condition, hides stretched tight as bow strings over their bones. A remnant of people walked down the road listlessly, to God knows where. They looked like ghosts, black skins camouflaged by a layer of dust. I could not imagine where they were headed in these parched conditions; perhaps anywhere seemed a better choice than the dry hell they were in now. Many were undoubtedly trying to get home to their villages, searching desperately for water and grass along the way. Mostly nomads through necessity, they foraged out from more or less permanent villages into the desert as the need arose. Others, true nomads, perhaps for centuries, traveled perpetually with their herds. Farming was non-existent in this arid land. Small gardens grow in good times, but there are no significant crops.

Cattle fare poorly in such a harsh climate. Unlike many wild animals who can survive extended periods with little or no water, cattle must drink almost daily. Because of the regular need for water and the excessive amount of grazing land required per head, cattle make an uneconomic food source all over the world. Much of the Western desert in America was once a thriving grassland teeming with game before it was decimated by livestock belonging to huge greedy cattle syndicates.

Cattle in Africa remain, however, a prime source of food and the chief means of barter. Traditionally, in some tribes like the Maasai, Samburu and Turkana, a man's wealth, importance, power and status in the tribe is determined by the number of cattle in his herd. Bloody inter-tribal wars still erupt when a few head of cattle are stolen in a raid.

The Maasai and the Samburu subsist basically on beef, milk, blood and the few berries or greens that they can gather. Most Africans reject game meat as being inferior to beef. Indigenous wild game animals can survive days without water. They have built-in genetic mechanisms for conserving body water during periods of limited water intake. In fact, wild animals have an adjustable thermostat so that their body temperature actually varies to accommodate the existing air temperature. When it is hot, their body temperature rises. When it is cold, it drops. In this way the demand for water intake decreases during hot days.

It is this same water conservation ability that makes the camel such a favorite of desert nomads, although camels are by no means as hardy in this respect as wild animals. In East Africa, camels are used mostly as pack animals for transporting goods. Since they are such a vital source of transportation, they are sacrificed for their meat only in extreme circumstances.

I knew of the drought before setting out on this trip, but I didn't begin to appreciate the seriousness or the reality of it until I saw it with my own eyes. Canvas water bags hung from the brush guards and fenders of the car—as much as we could carry. We knew that very little water was available along the Marsabit Road once we were north of the Samburu Game Reserve. Often there was not enough for the livestock. The extra water that we brought proved to be worth its weight in diamonds.

Small groups of people along the roadside, some with starving animals, became more frequent as we traveled north. Gracefully waving their wasted arms which protruded from emaciated bodies, they peered at us through eyes sunk deep in hollow sockets and pleaded with us to stop. Waving gourds and battered cups, they begged for water. The children had the typical bloated belly and brown-red skin of kwashiorkor, the protein deficiency of starvation, and stood listlessly by the road, too weak to wave. In later years, millions of people all over the world were introduced through television to starving African children in Ethiopia, Somalia, the Sudan and Rwanda. It was, however, my first introduction to the tragedy of starving children and it devastated my psyche for weeks to come, and lingers to this day. The scene was seared into my mind. I wondered what the kids on Park and 72nd Street were eating that night.

I couldn't avoid comparing my affluent, well-fed, well-schooled, comfortable teen-age patients in New York with the pitiful sights before me. The stark contrast was disturbing. Of course, comparisons of this sort are unrealistic and unfair, but hard to suppress. Life is unfair. It is obviously better to be one of the lucky ones, pick the right parents and have the right genes. How could God be so perverse? It's a question undoubtedly asked since the beginning of human history.

Our water supply was rapidly being exhausted and we realized that we must ration what little we had left. At the rate we were giving it out, it would not last. We couldn't be sure how much water supply remained at Marsabit. We assumed Lake Paradise was not dry, but there was no way to know for sure. Presumably there would be enough water in the lake, at least for drinking purposes. As we drew closer to Marsabit we saw large tanker trucks hauling water from the lake, headed for village tanks in a few favored locations. These trucks only added to our apprehension. How much would be left? I had never before faced a situation where such a basic and primary decision had to be made.

At midday we drove off the main road in search of shade. A single scrawny thorn acacia in a dry sand river provided some meager shelter for our lunch. We pulled up next to it and parked. A group of Samburu men and women, who had been invisible from the road, their camels laden with their worldly possessions, were digging in the sand a short way up the river bed. Several dry excavations pockmarked the river floor, mute testimony to the futility of their efforts to find water. Nan and I walked up the river bed to get a better view to see what they were doing.

With makeshift shovels fashioned from gourds and tin cups, they were scooping sand from a hole about four feet deep. As they dug, the sand persisted in flowing back into the hole. This was a difficult job with such crude tools. One of the holes, about six feet deep, was already completed. A puddle of dark brown, fetid water lined the bottom of the hole for a depth of several inches. I would have to be on the edge of death before I would drink it. Buckets fashioned from cowhide were used to haul this foul mixture of sand and water from the bottom of the well. Ghastly as it was, the camels and people were drinking it with relish.

An exquisite Samburu girl of about fifteen or sixteen watched us intently as we approached the group. With the classic delicate features of a pure Samburu, she was a knockout by anyone's standards. The Samburu, descendants from the Nilotic tribes of the north, migrated to Kenya from Egypt centuries ago. Her features, in contrast to Bantu people's, resembled those of pictographs on Egyptian tombs: wide-set, large eyes, aquiline nose with delicate arching nostrils and full, but not large lips. Her clean-shaven scalp identified her as an unmarried maiden. A bird-shaped tin ornament glistened from the middle of her forehead, suspended from a head band of multi-colored beads.

A sarong of thinly pounded animal skin, hung low around her pelvis, was her sole piece of clothing. Her pubescent breasts were small and perfectly formed. The skin of her slightly protuberant belly was unmarked by pregnancy striae. Despite the drought, she did not appear to be malnourished. Her sexual appeal was oddly heightened by the fine white layer of dust that coated her entire, almost naked, body.

Jewelry made from found metals and beads adorned her fingers and toes. The rings were fashioned from bent nails, copper wire and bits of leather thong. Hundreds of strands of multi-colored beads strung on copper wire circled her neck giving it an elongated appearance. The beads were gifts intended as a symbol of courtship from serious admirers. Samburu men add beads to the collection until their women have enough beads to support their heads, an indication of the wealth of the man or the ardor of a suitor. These enormous necklaces were never removed. Beaded loops hung from perforations in the upper portion of her ears. Beaded and copper bracelets adorned both wrists and ankles.

Watching Nan's every move, the young girl seemed fascinated. Truly rural Samburu are characteristically shy around strangers, especially Caucasians; however, this young woman seemed unintimidated by us. Photographs are usually forbidden by the Samburu, believing that a picture captures their soul. Sometimes bribery helps. Much as we wanted a picture of her and her group, we kept our cameras hidden, not wishing to further distress these people who were trying so desperately to survive.

With growing curiosity the girl came closer for a more detailed inspection. She had the innocent arrogance of a true nomad, untarnished by urban exposure. The Samburu considered themselves to be superior to everyone else. In fact, they pitied us because we had the misfortune not to be born as one of them. Nan, as usual in Africa, and despite previous problems with her attire, was dressed in khaki pants and shirt, a safari visor and no jewelry except for a wedding band and a cheap Casio wrist watch. Her hair was cut boyishly short. The young girl's fixation on Nan soon became apparent. She was clearly not afraid of us. The expression on the girl's face expressed the pity she felt as she examined Nan ever more closely.

Summoning all of her courage, the girl reached out and touched Nan on the shoulder, and finally on her breast. Nan's watch and simple wedding band were examined in detail. Her eyes swept over every inch of Nan's unadorned body. She then pointed to her own heavily jeweled anatomy. Her message was clear: Thank God I am a Samburu and can dress up properly and show how beautiful and desirable I am. I will surely attract an important warrior as a husband. With signs and motions, she made it clear that she wished to trade for the ring and watch. We gave her a drink of water instead.

Each of us views the world according to our own experience. Here we had met a girl in the desolate desert of Kenya in the middle of a devastating drought, digging cupfuls of putrid water from the bottom of a dried-up river bed, in order to survive. But despite her circumstances, she was still very much aware of her own sexual identity and the image she projected. Her vanity had not left her even in those adverse conditions. Her innate sense of competition with other women had not been dulled. All in all, I thought, she was no different from any other self-confident woman on Park Avenue, Rodeo Drive, or the Champs Elysée. I thought of some of the women that I saw in New York, pampered, spoiled, self-centered, desperately clutching at every means to salvage their aging physical charms. In the years since, I have often wondered what happened to that beautiful young woman.

12

Anne Spoerry: Mama Daktari

I was beginning my preoperative examination of the patients selected for surgery at the Marsabit Hospital in the north of Kenya. The first patient was placed in my arms by Dr. Anne Spoerry. It was a small baby with the exquisite features of a Somali, spoiled only by the fact that her entire scalp from her ears upwards was gangrenous—an ugly black thick crust. I had never seen anything like this. I wondered what on earth could have happened to produce such a horrendous wound in a baby. Anne explained to me that the mother, a lovely Somali woman, had placed her six-week-old baby on the ground. A well-camouflaged puff adder, one of the most poisonous snakes in Africa, was disturbed from its slumber in the thick dust, and struck, injecting its venom into the infant's scalp. Although critically ill for many days, miraculously, the baby survived the assault. However, her scalp above the ears had turned completely gangrenous. It was indeed a mystery how she had lived through such an injection of snake venom so close to the brain without early treatment by anti-venom. Perhaps the snake did not discharge its entire load of venom, injecting only a partial dose on the first strike as a warning. Or maybe the barrier provided by the bony skull protected her to some degree, serving as a shield for her brain. She was undernourished and anemic as a result of the toxin. The resilience of this infant was staggering. Dr. Spoerry always seemed to come up with the most extraordinary surgical problems.

As the doors of the Flying Doctor's hangar were slowly opened, the interior became flooded like a cathedral with the brilliant rays of the Kenya sun—someone said that it seemed as if the doors of heaven had opened for Dr. Anne Spoerry. Except for the Piper Lance, 5Y-AZT, belonging to her, all airplanes of the Flying Doctors had been removed from the hangar which was filled to overflowing with almost a thousand people, black, white, and brown, and was decorated with exotic leaves and brilliant red flowers. The life of the famous "Mama Daktari", Dr. Anne Spoerry, was being celebrated following her death at the age of 80 in 1999 after a career with the Flying Doctors of Africa that spanned more than three decades.

Anne was beloved by her African patients and her many friends. Before and after eulogies by Bethuel Kiplagat, the Chairman of AMREF, Eunice Kiereni, the Chairman of the Flying Doctors' Society, and myself, the Kenya National Choir sang a mixture of spirituals and traditional African songs. Suddenly, an unscheduled speaker arose, a tall dignified Kenyan, dressed in the simple clothes of a rural African. Speaking in a soft, barely audible voice, he delivered a brief, heartfelt message of love and farewell to Anne spoken, he said, on behalf of the many Africans who loved her. He wanted to be sure that her constituency was properly represented at her funeral.

After the eulogies, four pilots carried Anne's casket to her plane. As they proceeded, people covered the casket and the plane with flowers. The choir continued singing as it followed the plane being wheeled through the hangar doors to the edge of the tarmac. The crowd, singing along with the choir, moved as a mass following the plane. The chief of Aviation, Jim Heather-Hayes, climbed into the pilot's seat, started the engine, and as he taxied to the end of the runway for take-off, everyone waved and sang good-bye to Anne. There was not a dry eye in the mourning crowd. After take-off, and with permission of the tower, Jim buzzed the crowd, the wheels of the plane almost touching the roof of the hangar in one last good-bye. No film company could have staged a more beautiful and spectacular ceremony.

Jim flew Anne's casket to the port of Manda near the ancient Arab town of Lamu on the coast where Anne had conducted regular clinics amongst the local tribes for many years. A crowd of somber and weeping people, Arab and African, met the plane and carried her remains to her final resting place.

Anne was a living legend, one of the most admired and beloved persons in East Africa. An impressive woman with the bronzed, weather-beaten face of a Montana rancher, Anne spent her life out of doors, working on her farm, flying around Africa and visiting the many remote hospitals and mobile clinics that depended on her for medical care. Etched with fine wrinkles and "smile" lines radiating from her eyes and mouth, she exuded an aura of no-nonsense authority wherever she worked. She spoke in a short clipped cadence. Always outspoken, Anne complained in plain language about the condition of airstrips, the shortcomings of air traffic controllers, mechanics, bureaucrats, politicians and anything else that did not measure up to her expectations. One always knew where Anne stood on any subject.

Spurning dresses, except on special occasions, she favored bush shirts, pants, vests, and suede chukka boots. The winged insignia of the Flying Doctors was always fixed to her shirt, Anne cut a colorful figure wherever she went. Half-glasses swinging from a lanyard around her neck, when not perched on the end of her nose. As a practical matter, an unruly topknot of speckled gray hair was cut boyishly short—she had little truck with vanity. An aviator's baseball cap was often perched on top of her head. Her restless energy belied her eighty years.

Hair-raising experiences in the hostile back country were common fare for Anne, affectionately known as "Mama Daktari" by her many African patients. Her regular clinic rounds included some of the most hazardous and remote regions in Africa, often amongst bandit-infested country in the northern provinces of Kenya bordering on Ethiopia, Somalia, and the Sudan, as well as several clinics near Lamu on the coast. In addition to English, which she spoke with a just tinge of a Gallic accent, and French, her mother tongue, she was fluent in Swahili and spoke a considerable amount of Maasai as well, learned during her many years of conducting mobile clinics in Masailand. This extraordinary woman underwent a total hip replacement in 1994, and despite advice to the contrary, was flying her plane on regular bush rounds six weeks later. Anne regularly visited Marsabit Hospital, one of the several clinics and hospitals on her route in northern Kenya. She often flew alone or occasionally with a nurse or specialist outreach surgeon. She traveled light with a black bag and vital signs instruments, emergency kit with operating instruments, and various medications.

Her case load included such rarities as lion mauling, spear and rifle wounds, mental illness, tuberculosis, amebic colitis, dehydration, malaria, epilepsy, snake bites, pregnancies, and *njaa* (hunger).

A native of Cannes, southern France, Dr. Spoerry obtained her M.D. at the Faculté de Médecine in Paris, during World War II. She had been a member of the French resistance, and was eventually caught by the Nazis and incarcerated in Ravensbruck, the infamous concentration camp. She managed to survive until the end of the war. After the war, fed up with Europe, Anne migrated to Africa. Africa bewitched her at first sight and she became determined to settle there and practice medicine. After considerable difficulty with the Immigration Department and the details of moving, Anne made her home in Subukia in rural Kenya where she became a farmer and a general practitioner. She cared for the local Kikuyu people at the government clinic at Ol Kalou in the Rift Valley where she practiced for fourteen years.

Anne became used to grisly scenes during the Mau Mau rebellion in Ol Kalou, similar to those she had witnessed in occupied Europe. She cared for whites and Africans alike. Danger was no stranger to her.

Practicing as a rural doctor and farming did not satisfy her restless nature, so in 1963 at the age of forty-five and on a whim, she learned to fly, beginning a lifelong love affair with airplanes. It became her dream to marry flying with medicine which she did for the rest of her life. Anne knew of the Flying Doctors and was acquainted with Mike Wood. She vowed to find a way to work with the Flying Doctors. It took a lot of persuading for us to accept her as part of the team, largely because at that time money was short and we could not afford to pay her a salary. There was also concern that flying to remote areas to service bush clinics was a dangerous occupation, possibly not suited for a woman in Africa; however, given her history, it was clear that she was not one to be put off by dangerous situations. Anne's persistence prevailed and she joined the Flying Doctors in 1965. She carried on her work until her death.

The year before Anne died, I joined her on a clinic visit to Loliondo in northern Tanzania. Shortly after take-off she turned the controls of her Piper Lance over to me after first giving me a compass heading to the mission hospital. For the hour and few minutes it took for the flight, Anne constantly heckled me to maintain a constant altitude and a steady compass course. "My God but you are rusty," she said, "can't you fly this thing straight and level?" It was all good natured fun between two old friends, and I look back on that last trip with immense pleasure.

In the north of Kenya, visible for miles around, an enigmatic mountain massif rises from the arid flat desert floor like a medieval castle, the result of an ancient volcanic eruption—Marsabit. For centuries it has been an active trading center where goods of every description were bartered by Turkana, Samburu, Somalis, Arabs, and Ethiopians. Until slavery was abolished in the mid-nineteenth century, Arab caravans passed through Marsabit from the interior on their way to seaports in the north, where their human cargo was sold and shipped to Europe and the Americas. Poachers still smuggle ivory, rhino horns, colobus monkey skins, and other illegal products through Marsabit for sale in Asia and the Middle East where they are much valued as objects d'art. Despite the ban in recent years, ivory fetches a huge price in the Middle and Far East where it is used for carving. Rhino horn is greatly favored for dagger handles in Arabian countries and the powdered horn is used as an aphrodisiac in the Far East.

Marsabit was a favorite hunting area for Ernest Hemingway, Robert Ruark, Carl Akley and other big game hunters who wrote of their experiences there. Their books became familiar to a generation of armchair explorers. Greater kudu, leopards, lions, rhinos and the largest elephants in the world roamed the forests and savannahs of Marsabit until virtually exterminated by poachers in recent years. Hemingway wrote *The Green Hills of Africa* from his camp near Marsabit. Ahmed, for many years the largest elephant in the world, whose enormous tusks were so long and heavy that they rested on the ground, was protected by armed guards and decreed a national treasure by President Jomo Kenyatta of Kenya. Ahmed died a natural death, escaping poachers, and his huge body is visible today in the National Museum in Nairobi. The elephant population is now beginning to recover, but no longer are the huge tusks of yesteryear seen. Marsabit is still wild Africa at its most colorful, a trip to the past.

I visited Marsabit several times on surgical safaris. It is one of my favorite places in Africa. On my first visit there with Nan, several years after our initial visit to Kaimosi, we undertook a surgical safari that began at Maralal, where we found our old friend Dr. Peter Green (from Kaimosi) in charge. It was at Maralal that I first saw a young boy who had lost his hand to the jaws of a hungry hyena. Several years later, Dr. Bill Adams-Ray (then the reconstructive surgeon at AMREF) and I operated on a young boy at Moshi (see photographs) who had lost both hands to the wrist to a hyena while protecting his father's goats. He did not wish to face his father's fury if he lost one of the animals to the hyena. We constructed a pincer, much like a lobster claw, using both bones of one forearm with which he could hold things and even write his name with a pen. Later, Dr. Adams-Ray did a similar operation on the remaining forearm. The horrors of the ongoing war in Sierra Leone have left hundreds of people without hands, enough to keep many surgeons busy for many years.

I operated for four days at Maralal with a characteristic list of patients. We then joined Monty Ruben at Samburu to continue our journey on to Marsabit where we camped at Lake Paradise; part work and part R & R. From this base I could perform surgery at the hospital of Marsabit as well as explore the surrounding countryside. I had operated there the previous year with Mike Wood and Anne Spoerry and I was eager to see the results of our surgery if the patients could still be located.

The view from our campsite at Lake Paradise was unequaled anywhere on earth. The mountain surrounding the lake was blanketed with primeval forest extending down into the crater to the shores of the lake. Wildlife abounded in the forest and surrounding area. The forest teemed with many species of birds, many of them winter migrants from Europe. An avid bird watcher, Nan reveled in this visual feast of colorful birds. Luckily, we found and photographed Ahmed and his giant protector, Abdullah, shortly before the magnificent old elephant died.

Martin and Osa Johnson, a famous exploring team popular in the 1920s and 1930s based their camp at Lake Paradise, a clear, freshwater lake which lies in a volcanic crater in the forests of Marsabit. From their camp they explored much of this region by car and a specially equipped amphibious plane. The Johnsons wrote books and produced some of the earliest films about Africa for the lecture circuit in Europe and America. Countless thousands were stimulated by their adventures. By today's standards, their attitude toward the Africans was naive and politically unacceptable, but at that time their explorations were eagerly followed by the Western world.

We were glad to see that the tankers transporting water to the drought-ridden northern province had not significantly depleted the lake, there was still plenty of sparkling clear water. Shortly after making camp, Rob Glen, the renowned African sculptor, and Peter Jenkins, a top-notch game warden, emerged from the forest where they had been netting birds, both resident and migratory as part of an ongoing study. We enjoyed a peaceful evening drink by the fire, swapping stories with Peter and Rob, both of whom had a vast knowledge of the wildlife to be found at Marsabit.

For two days we explored, tracked game and took many photographs. The hospital and my work beckoned, so on the third morning I began the operating schedule previously arranged by radio with the Flying Doctors headquarters in Nairobi. Gracious and ever helpful, the Anglican nuns who staffed the hospital (it has since been taken over by the government), accompanied me on rounds to review the patients scheduled for surgery. Dr. Anne Spoerry had selected many of the patients on her last visit. Measuring the time available, I made a final selection of patients that I could reasonably expect to operate on during this trip.

The surgical list included the baby with gangrene of the scalp following the puff adder bite I mentioned at the beginning of this chapter; three Turkana men with huge hydatid cysts of the liver; a Somali with a colostomy who had been gored by a buffalo; two cleft lip patients; a man with scar deformities of the eyelids; a patient with major head trauma following a bicycle accident and a young Samburu woman with severe scarring of the vaginal opening following ritual genital mutilation.

I decided to start with the baby. It was imperative to remove the dead scalp tissue before infection set in. Before undertaking the surgery, however, the anemia had to be reversed with a blood transfusion. Fortunately, the laboratory at Marsabit confirmed that the mother's blood was a compatible match and the baby was transfused prior to surgery. Blood transfusion does not correct malnutrition although it is helpful. High caloric diet and time were required to correct this problem. Removal of the gangrenous tissue was the first step in paving the way for eventual healing. Skin grafts would follow to cover the open wound. Not a happy choice, but the only option available. An infection would surely kill her in such a weakened condition.

The operating theater at Marsabit was in a small building which also contained a utility room and scrub sinks. Light was provided by daylight, and an electric spotlight powered by an old generator. An ancient autoclave, wheezing and hissing, effectively sterilized the instruments. The operating room nurse and an assistant were hard working, good natured and eager to please. A nurse from the wards administered general anesthesia with a machine that delivered a mixture of oxygen and ether. Operating here was a pleasure for me. The *esprit de corps* amongst the staff in bush hospitals is usually excellent. Everyone pulls together as a team to do the best possible job, often under adverse conditions and many limitations. Surprisingly, the operative mortality rate and incidence of infection is generally low in bush hospitals, possibly because of the innate toughness of the African patient who, after surviving a childhood fraught with danger from diseases of every description likely, develops a vigorous natural immunity against bacteria.

The ritual of scrubbing affords the surgeon a few minutes to review his surgical plan and consider all options available to him. As I scrubbed and prepared to operate on this baby, I contrasted the ritual with scrubbing for an operation in New York. At this primitive hospital, in the heart of Africa, a positive, cheerful attitude prevailed. The tasks that would occupy an army of OR personnel in New York were efficiently handled by two or three people. There were no personality clashes, no egos jockeying for position—only the task at hand was important. Saving that child was the focus of all activity.

I was exhilarated. Much like the captain of a ship, I was absolutely in charge and responsible. The sole desire of everyone on the team was to save the baby. In New York, I would be only one cog in a complicated machine. Perhaps the bush surgeon is compensated for a lonely life devoid of the customary honors and accolades of an urban career knowing that he, and he alone, often holds the power of life or death in his hands. Financial security and material gains are limited for the doctor working in the Third World. Having tasted the rewards of being a bush surgeon from time to time, I often wondered if I had the disposition and discipline required to make it a full-time job.

The baby was put to sleep under a light ether anesthesia and the gangrenous scalp dissected away from the underlying skull. Blood loss during surgery was minimal and replaced by further blood transfusion. A healthy layer of "proud flesh" (granulation tissue) was revealed covering the skull upon removal of the gangrenous tissue. Granulation tissue or proud flesh is an indication that the body is attempting to heal the wound. Such tissue is rich in small blood vessels (capillaries) necessary for new skin to grow. Therefore, it is an ideal bed upon which to apply a skin graft, which in this case was planned in a second operation, providing an interval for improving the cleanliness of the wound to assure success of a skin graft. The baby recovered from the anesthetic without incident. Afterward I as was able to follow her progress by radio from Flying Doctors' headquarters in Nairobi. Dr. Anne Spoerry filled me in on the details of her healing. The superb nursing staff at Marsabit Hospital kept the wound clean with saline dressings. Fortuitously, Dr. David Furnas, a plastic surgeon from California on his annual trip to Kenya to work with the Flying Doctors, visited Marsabit a month later. He covered the large scalp wound with a skin graft from the baby's buttocks. The graft healed well.

Huge hydatid cysts of the internal organs, particularly the liver, result from infestation by dog tapeworm and are endemic amongst the Turkana and other herdsmen of northern Kenya. The causative organism, *Echinococcus granulosis*, exists primarily in the intestinal tracts of canines, and commonly infests humans who live in intimate contact with infected dogs. The dogs are useful to herd livestock. The children, in particular live in close contact with their dogs. Eggs from the parasite are expelled in the feces of the dog and human infestation occurs through direct hand to mouth contact or by ingesting contaminated food or water in adults.

After the parasite's eggs penetrate the wall of the intestines they migrate to various organs where they colonize and form cysts. These cysts can occur anywhere in the body but have a predilection for the lungs, liver, brain and bone. Many years may be required to form cysts which, in some cases, become enormous. Starvation and death can occur if the cysts become so large that they interfere with organ function. Such large cysts require surgical drainage, a common operation in the north of Kenya.

Carefully, I drained the huge cyst of the liver in my patient at Marsabit, to prevent spillage of the contents into the abdominal cavity. Evacuation of these large growths is not generally life-threatening, but it is a major procedure, nevertheless. Recurrence of cysts is common because the patients frequently become reinfected. Also, if the contents of the cyst are spilled into the abdominal cavity during surgery, the parasites form other cysts. Doctors often delay surgical drainage of hydatid cysts until or unless pressure symptoms become severe, or life is threatened. In my patient, chronic pain and weight loss caused by the cyst had become debilitating.

I connected the two ends of the colostomy in the patient who had been gored by the buffalo to re-establish the continuity of the intestinal tract. The operation was relatively simple and went well.

The man injured when he and his bicycle collided with a telegraph pole proved a difficult problem. A large splinter of wood had penetrated his eye socket severing the muscles and tendon that raise the eyelid, so that the lid hung like a curtain. Fortunately the globe of the eye was not penetrated. He was blind in the eye because he could not open the lid. Removal of the wooden splinter and repair of the muscles and tendon required delicate and time-consuming dissection to avoid injury to the eye itself. I learned later from Anne Spoerry that the operation was successful. The wound healed without incident and with normal vision in the operated eye.

The young woman who suffered severe scarring from ritual genital mutilation had formed a web of scar tissue across the lips of her genitalia, compromising the opening of her vagina. I excised the scar tissue and reconstructed the vaginal opening with flaps of skin brought in from her inner thigh much like the technique I had employed at Kaloleni Hospital many years before. I then applied free skin grafts to cover the raw area left on her thighs. This Samburu woman had been circumcised when she was in her early teens. The extensive scar tissue surrounding her vagina made intercourse impossible; nevertheless, a young man wanted to marry her. I hoped that the operation would make intercourse, and therefore marriage, possible. I later learned from Dr. Spoerry that the operation had indeed been a success and that the young woman was able to marry her Samburu warrior.

After three days of surgery, we returned to Nairobi. I often think of mysterious Marsabit, the long dusty road leading to it, and the terrible drought that year which was finally ended when the rains came in April. But most of all I think about Dr. Anne Spoerry, whom I loved dearly, during the many years we were associated as colleagues and close friends.

13

Royal Encounter

Monster crocodiles and the largest freshwater fish in the world, the huge Nile Perch, reside in Lake Turkana. Nestled in the Rift Valley in the northwestern corner of Kenya, the lake lies in a north-south direction with the northern end resting in Ethiopia. It is 155 miles long, 2,471 square miles in area, and quite shallow. A single river, the Omo, feeds the lake from the White Nile. Having no outlet, the water is brackish, an ideal environment for crocodiles, fish, hippos and many species of birds.

Count Teleki explored the shores of the lake in 1886 and named it Lake Rudolf, in honor of the crown Prince of Austria. However, the name Lake Turkana is preferred by most. Important hominid fossils were discovered along the shore of the lake by Richard Leakey including "Turkana Boy," a nearly complete skeleton 1.6 million years old, altering the predominant view of human evolution. The jade green color of the water prompted early travelers to adopt the name "Jade Sea." A few nomads and the Turkana tribe inhabit the arid desert which surrounds the lake. The Turkana raise livestock and harvest fish. The fish, an excellent source of protein, are dried by the sun on wooden racks and sold in the open marketplaces of Kenya.

Centers of civilization are few and far between in this punishing environment, where daytime temperatures often reach 110 degrees F. Lodwar, a township and medical base, is a rare hub of activity on the west side of the lake. Before the Global Positioning System of navigation by satellite fix, international and local flights depended on the VOR navigational system at Lodwar to navigate to and from Nairobi and Entebbe. It was the only navigational aid for hundreds of miles in any direction. A small hospital and clinic, visited by the Flying Doctors, meets the medical needs of the region. Very large hydatid cysts are common amongst the Turkana who visit the clinic. The surgical schedule is usually filled with other more common surgical problems, too, such as hernia, prostatic hypertrophy, amputations, vesico-vaginal fistulas, hydrocele and osteomyelitis.

In 1971, after operating for several days at Lodwar, I joined Nan and her brother, "Major Bowes," and her sister-in-law, Di, for a weekend of fishing at the Lake Turkana Fishing Lodge, at Ferguson's Gulf. After completing my operating schedule, Jim Heather-Hayes, then the chief pilot of the Flying Doctors, picked me up at Lodwar. Nan and the others were already on board the plane. "It was bloody difficult getting you reservations in the camp," said Jim on the short flight over. "I don't know why, but when we radioed we were first told that no reservations were available. I put some pressure on and finally got you some accommodation, but only after a real third degree about who you are, where you are from and who you represent." The Cessna bucked and bounced unmercifully in the turbulence of midday as we descended through the thermals towards the dirt airstrip of the fishing camp.

Jim was born in London in 1947, but raised in Africa from the age of fourteen months. He became enamored with flying as a very young man and attained his private pilot's license with the sum total of 75 hours in 1967, almost a record. He joined the Flying Doctors shortly after obtaining his private license. Except for a short spell as a charter pilot (which he found boring), he has been flying with us ever since. He became chief pilot, and later aviation manager, and finally aviation director, a job he still holds. Jim is a tall handsome man, six feet two inches tall, with a ruddy complexion and sandy blond hair. He has an easy manner and is respected by all who have worked with and for him. He will fly anywhere and anytime to rescue a patient in need.

Nan commented that she found it odd after surveying the camp below that she could not see any people. The camp looked deserted. At that time of year, the camp should be full of fishermen. I thought that it was probably full, but that the people were out on the lake fishing for the day. A cloud of white dust spewed from the tail as we landed. Robin Anderson, the camp manager and an old friend of ours, met us in an ancient Land Rover that rattled the short distance to the camp.

The lodge at Ferguson's Gulf consisted of a series of cabins built on a spit of land extending out into the lake. A somewhat larger building constituted the camp headquarters. "Where is everybody?" I asked. "Out fishing," said Robin without further explanation.

While unpacking our gear Nan asked if I had noticed the tall antennas on the compound. I had, and we couldn't imagine why Robin would need more than one radio antenna for a fishing camp. There were four others almost the same in height. I wondered if they were some sort of government installation.

My brother-in-law, Major, and I were eager to try our hand at catching the fabled tiger fish, one of the great fighting fishes of the world. As soon as we finished unpacking, we gathered some spinning rods, reels and lures from the gear closet of the lodge, and headed for the beach. There was still no one in sight. A giant swirl and a splash greeted my lure almost the second it hit the water, as a tiger fish charged the flashing metal. Immediately the line became taught with a jerk, the rod bent almost double, and line began to strip from the reel as the fish dashed for deeper water. A twenty-minute fight finished with the beaching of a ten-pound fish, with as vicious a set of teeth as I had ever seen.

After a time I joined Major, who beckoned from further down the shoreline. "Look at these bones," he said. "Are they human?" Sure enough, we were looking at several human bones strewn for some distance along the shore. I recognized pieces of several long bones: femurs, tibiae, humerus and the remnants of pelvic bones, but no skulls. I couldn't imagine what had happened here short of a battle of some kind. As we were examining the bones, three young African boys ran down the beach toward us shouting "*Mamba, mamba, mamba.*" My Swahili was scanty; the only "mamba" I knew of was a snake, and none was in sight.

Adding to the confusion of looking at human bones and trying to understand the consternation of the boys, a small boat hove into view heading for the rickety dock that extended out into the lake for a distance of about twenty feet. I gathered my fishing equipment and headed for the dock, leaving the mysteries of the bones and *mamba* behind for the time being. I hoped to see the catch and to learn the details of the day's fishing out on the lake, since we were planning to fish on the following day.

The boat chugged to a stop, tied up alongside the dock and two khaki-clad men emerged from the small cabin in the front. Both looked northern European, one with blond hair and the other with a shock of red. They were sunburned, the redhead with a fresh crop of freckles. One wore a sidearm which I recognized as an English Webley revolver. Both men looked at me with expressionless but not unfriendly faces, but offered no greeting.

"How did you do?" I asked, "Catch any fish?" Neither answered me. I guessed they might be Scandinavian or perhaps German and possibly did not understand English. Rods and reels were stowed shipshape in brackets along the gunwale of the boat, but no fish were to be seen. Feeling awkward, a dignified retreat seemed prudent. While pondering this embarrassing problem, I caught sight of another boat approaching the dock from the opposite side. I decided that I had just as well wait and see who these people were. I hoped they would be more communicative than those in the first boat.

As the boat came closer, I could see two more men in the open cockpit at the rear of the boat, also dressed in khaki, both bearing sidearms, one with a machine gun hanging from his shoulder. They kept a close eye on me while the boat tied up at the dock. I was about to ask them about fishing, when a third man, carrying a portable radio and a black case emerged from the cabin. A fourth, slightly built young man in khaki, wearing a bush hat and dark sunglasses, soon followed.

"Good afternoon, Sir," I said, "did you have any luck." "Fantastic day," he answered, "Just look at these two perch." He spoke with an aristocratic British accent, pulling back the edge of a tarpaulin beneath which were two giant Nile Perch. "What wonderful luck." I said. "We are fishing for them tomorrow, and I only hope we have as much luck as you."

While we were talking, the other three men were busy loading the black boxes and the fishing gear onto the dock, all the while watching me. I suddenly realized that I was talking to Charles, Prince of Wales. Dumbstruck, I searched for words. I had met enough celebrities in my life not to be at a total loss, but here, quite out of context, was Prince Charles himself in the wilds of the northern frontier of Kenya, talking to me about fishing.

Although I had never met him in person, I knew that Prince Charles had become a patron of the Flying Doctors. In fact, one of his tasks while on his visit to Kenya was to dedicate our new hangar at Wilson Airport. We talked fishing as we walked the short distance to the lodge together. Fisherman communicate in an international language of their own, and we shared fishing stories as we walked. Big game hunting appalled him. He considered those who did it to be uninformed bores with no heart and little feeling about the animals that they "murder" with telescopic sights and high-powered rifles. I shared fly fishing stories of my youth while growing up in the Rocky Mountains. It was a warm and friendly conversation.

As we parted, Prince Charles invited me and my party to join him for evening cocktails on the terrace before dinner. I readily accepted. Nan was duly excited about the news and especially that we were going to have our evening drink with the Prince. "That explains all of the radio antennas around the camp." she noted. After showering, we joined Major and Di and wandered over to the terrace where Prince Charles and his party of some twenty men were already gathered, sipping drinks.

Prince Charles graciously kissed the hands of the ladies and shook hands with Major as I introduced them. He explained that he was at the end of a walking safari with camels in the desert. He was scheduled to return to England the next day. Accompanying him on the trip were his bodyguards, communications expert, various friends and a few military types. He told Nan and her very attractive sister-in-law Di, that he was bored with the constant company of men and was truly glad to see two beautiful women.

He was enthusiastic about being a patron of the Flying Doctors and had many questions about us and our plans, which I was delighted to answer. With the temperature still hovering around 100 degrees, the red ball of the sun sank into the lake. Two dinner tables had been set on the terrace, a smaller one for me and my party and a large one, parallel to ours, for the Prince and his entourage. The Prince and his party had created a considerable stir behind the scenes at the fishing camp, which had never been graced by royalty before.

Extra cooks and waiters had been recruited from the town of Isiolo, along with a pleasant woman to oversee the operation and ensure that things went smoothly. Despite the heat, this lady was dressed in a mid-calf, white satin, short-sleeved dress, complete with white pumps, nylon stockings and elbow-length kid gloves. She wore a string of pearls with earrings to match, and a white barrette in her hair. Constantly fussing with the place settings, admonishing the waiters and generally clucking about, she was clearly nervous about her assigned role.

In perfect hand-written script, the dinner was described on the menu and consisted of an appetizer of tilapia (a delicious fish) with cucumber sauce, followed by a main course of roast beef with horseradish sauce and Yorkshire pudding. Dessert was to be chocolate cake topped with whipped cream. A heavy red burgundy complimented the meal (but not the heat).

Being the smaller table of the two, ours was served first—an unexplainable breach of etiquette, I thought. The meal progressed smoothly. As the dishes were being cleared from the main course, Major tasted his desert. By hand signal he urgently summoned the hovering lady and announced that someone in the kitchen had mistakenly put the cucumber fish sauce on the chocolate surprise, and that Prince Charles was, at that moment, about to put a forkful of this ghastly mixture into his royal mouth.

Jet-propelled, the woman leaped the distance between the tables and grabbed the Prince's hand as he was about to plunge the cake into his mouth. Spluttering, she explained that he was about to eat chocolate cake with a topping of cucumber sauce instead of whipped cream.

The Prince's amazement at having his wrist grabbed so abruptly soon vanished. His good humor emerged when he laughed heartily at the mistake and soothed our very flustered hostess's feelings.

Dinner finished without further mishap, and we enjoyed coffee beneath the brilliant stars. We did not see the Prince the next morning. His party left at dawn. In fact, we did not see him again for nearly twenty years, until we attended the London premier of the movie *Out of Africa*, and stood in the receiving line for him and Princess Diana. Oddly enough he remembered me, and we relived our dinner party together on the shores of the lake.

At the request of Robin, the camp manager, I held a brief clinic early the following morning for some local Turkana with various medical problems. During the course of the clinic, I asked the meaning of *mamba*. In Swahili, *mamba* means crocodile, I was told, and the lake is full of giant crocs who often submerge near the shore waiting for unsuspecting humans to venture too close to the water. It was also a tribal tradition to drag the bodies of the dead to the shore where the *mamba* efficiently disposed of them—hence the human bones we had seen along the lakeshore.

We spent the remainder of the day catching several giant Nile Perch. We enjoyed a picnic lunch at Central Island where we saw dozens of huge crocodiles sunning themselves; some reaching lengths of eighteen feet. On the way back to the lodge we ran out of gas. "Because Prince Charles's people used it all up," we were told. We floated in the growing darkness for a couple of hours, surrounded by gleaming red spots—the eyes of the ever-vigilant *mambas*. The rescue boat eventually arrived and towed us in, ending an event-filled day.

14

A Weekend of Fire

Nan and I had been working in Nairobi for two weeks helping to organize the schedule of nine teams of plastic surgeons from America and Europe, recruited to begin the first stages of repairing the many Kenyans injured in the US Embassy bombing of August 7, 1998 in Nairobi. My longtime friend and Kenya "son," Jeremy Block, invited us to spend the weekend at his new ranch which we gratefully accepted. Jeremy had spent many weekends and holidays in our house in New York while he was attending school in America. Nan and I served as surrogate American parents at his father's request. We have been close friends ever since.

Late on the Friday afternoon Nan, Carolyn Fox and I helped Jeremy load his Cessna 206 with groceries, hand luggage and various new tools for the ranch. We eagerly looked forward to a relaxing weekend at Ole Naishu (Maasai for land of honey), his 35,000-acre cattle ranch in the beautiful open savannahs and mountains northwest of Mount Kenya. Carolyn, a beautiful and talented woman, had recently moved from her home in Edinburgh, Scotland to begin a new life with Jeremy in Kenya, and this was a chance for us to get acquainted.

Jeremy told us that 2,000 head of cattle grazed and roamed free on Ole Naishu. The acreage was an important link in a chain of private ranches joined for the purpose of re-establishing the ancient elephant migratory routes from the northern provinces of Kenya, south to the Mara River on the Tanzanian border. Poaching and encroachment by farms and ranches in recent years had severely compromised the migration route. Dedicated to preserving the elephants after many years of slaughter for their tusks, many people worked hard to re-establish this safe route. The famous wildlife preservation team of Ian and Oria Douglas-Hamilton worked ceaselessly in this endeavor, with the enthusiastic cooperation of adjoining ranchers.

The weekend promised to be especially interesting. Jeremy had invited the chiefs and headmen of the local tribes of Maasai, Eldorobo and Samburu to a meeting on the ranch as a gesture of friendship, and to inspire confidence in him as the new owner. He wished to pledge his cooperation with them, and to assure them that he would not interfere with their traditional way of life. They were welcome on the property provided they respected the livestock and forest. A sumptuous barbecue feast washed down with cold beer was to culminate the meeting. Jeremy was keen to establish friendly bonds with the locals.

Dry for many months without rain, the hot summer winds of Kenya created uncomfortable turbulence during the ninety-minute flight to the ranch. Numerous bush fires spewed columns of smoke into the sky from the parched grasslands below. The peaks of Mount Kenya emerged majestically above the clouds as we neared the ranch. The landscape, however, was partially obscured by five separate fires burning vigorously a few miles north of the ranch buildings.

Jeremy banked the plane in a tight circle over the blazing bush to get a clear picture of the extent of the fire and its direction. The view was alarming. Several small isolated groups of firefighters could be seen beating at the flames with huge brooms made of brush. Of course, no water was available and tanker planes were non-existent in this part of Kenya.

Jeremy was understandably worried, visualizing his dream of a cattle ranch literally going up in smoke. As we approached the rough landing strip near the house, he warned us to securely fasten our chest straps as well as our seat belts since the "ground effect" could increase the turbulence as we lost altitude. A vicious cross wind swept almost at right angles across the airstrip making the landing quite tricky. I was glad Jeremy was flying and not me. He executed a near perfect landing with full opposite controls (rudder and ailerons) touching down the upwind wheel first.

Ole Naishu's new ranch manager, Simon Dugdale, a lean, tall, blond New Zealander in his mid-twenties met us at the strip and walked us to the ranch house. Simon had left the fire and driven to the airstrip when he saw the plane approaching. He had worked on a farm in Tanzania for the last five years, fallen in love with Africa and planned to emigrate permanently to Kenya. Simon was concerned, but believed the fires to be still relatively under control. He and Barry Gaymer, who had flown up earlier that afternoon from Lake Naivasha, had worked out a plan to contain the fires, which they outlined to us.

Barry had flown to the farm to advise Jeremy on a myriad of matters pertaining to his new ranch. Every spare man was assigned to fire-fighting. To Jeremy's relief, the cattle herds in proximity to the fires had already been moved upwind to safe locations. The danger was there, but comforted by Simon's report, we settled down to an excellent ranch dinner to celebrate Valentine's Day weekend. Jeremy decided that to cancel the meeting and barbecue with the local Africans was premature at that point. He would wait and see what happened to the fires the following day.

Next morning, Saturday, was spent driving around the ranch with Jeremy, who proudly pointed out the topography of his new property and the several small herds of game that occupied it. We were able to observe the progress of the fires from the high ground along the mountain ridges. Later in the day, Jeremy and I went up in his Cessna, circled the fires and gave radio directions by walkie-talkie to the groups of firefighters below. The wind was still strong, around twenty knots and gusting to thirty, but the fires seemed to be contained. Of concern were two new fires on the side of a steep mountain with the wind blowing the flames up the slope of the mountainside. Several crew members were diverted to fight these new threats.

The evening meal was less jovial than on the previous night. There was now a growing realization that the fires might well get out of control unless the wind, which was still strong, abated. The grass had grown high as the result of the heavy and prolonged rains of the previous spring and early summer, but had become tinder-dry since. The unrelenting hot wind contributed to the situation. As a precaution, the owners of adjacent ranches were apprised by radio of the hazardous situation and the very real possibility that the fires could spread over the entire area.

We woke up on Valentine's morning to Simon's report that the fires were now raging out of control over several thousand acres. Some of the individual fires had coalesced and were advancing along a solid line up the mountain slopes in a westerly direction. It was now obvious that the meeting and the barbecue party had to be postponed, in spite of the fat steer that had been slaughtered and prepared for the fire pit. Many of the chiefs with their retinues had already arrived for the party. Many agreed to fight the fire, and did so throughout the day and following night with considerable stamina and bravery.

The work was hard and dirty. In the absence of water, the flames were fought by the age-old method of beating them out with branches cut from trees. The ranch tractor was in constant use ferrying firefighters to and from the fire line, now on the mountain top, and plowing fire breaks. During much of the morning, Jeremy directed the firefighters by radio from his plane. Many people from surrounding ranches arrived to help. The local police in Nanyuki and a British Army unit stationed several miles away were alerted and asked to lend a hand if possible.

At midday a frantic radio message was received from Barry Gaymer. Stephen, Jeremy's cook, had insisted on going to the fire line to help distribute drinking water and to be generally useful. Stephen was sitting on the front of the tractor on the way to the fire when the tractor hit a bump and he fell under a front wheel. He was unconscious. Barry said that the tire marks were clearly visible where they had passed over Stephen's pelvis. Barry was very concerned that Stephen had sustained a spinal injury. He did not dare move him.

Fearing that I was indeed dealing with a spinal injury, Carolyn, Nan and I split a bed board lengthwise to serve as a solid platform on which to immobilize Stephen. Clean sheets were cut into long strips to serve as straps. I carried morphine in my pack, but we had no apparatus suitable to properly immobilize a spinal injury. The bed board and sheet strips were loaded into the back of a Land Rover, and Jeremy and I set off for the mountain top about five miles away. The track was rough, steep and in some stretches consisted only of deep ruts dug by the wheels of the tractor on its journey to and from the fire line—definitely not an ideal road for transporting a possible spinal injury.

During our the trip up the mountain, Nan and Carolyn contacted Flying Doctors by radio and requested an emergency medical team. They reported that we had a possible spinal injury patient. Judy Wangai, the chief nurse on duty in the radio room, affirmed that a team would be sent immediately and that two aircraft were available that were capable of transporting a spinal injury, our Cessna twin-engine 402 and the pride of our fleet, a Cessna Grand Caravan. Nan related this news by walkie-talkie to us as we approached the accident site.

Neither Jeremy nor I thought that either the 402 or the Caravan had the capability of handling the short, rough airstrip at the ranch. Jeremy told the girls to inform the Flying Doctors that we would meet them at Nanyuki which had a commercial runway just a half-hour's flight from the ranch. We planned to take Stephen there in Jeremy's Cessna 206. I learned later to my chagrin that the Caravan was perfectly capable of landing on Jeremy's strip. Despite its size, it has excellent short-field capabilities. Considerable time and trouble could have been saved had we directed the team to fly to the ranch in the Caravan, a fantastic airplane ideal for bush work.

We also heard on the radio that Phil Mathews, an ex-Flying Doctors' pilot we have already met in Chapter Nine, was monitoring the fires in a small helicopter. Phil offered to try to land the chopper and pick up the patient, but I nixed the plan. I felt certain that Stephen, stretched out on the bed board, could not be fitted into the chopper. Further, from what we had learned of the accident site, even a chopper would have a difficult time finding space to land there.

Barry and several Africans were anxiously awaiting our arrival. Barry told us that Stephen had gained consciousness for a brief moment before slipping away into unconsciousness again. I found him lying on the road, shaded by some branches of a tree that had been rigged up by his companions. The tractor tire tracks were clearly visible passing over his upper thighs. There were no signs of shock, but I could get a response from him only with persistent questioning. I was able to determine that he could move his legs—a very good sign—and that he had sensation in both of them. A basic neurological exam elicited no abnormal reflexes, and there was no tenderness over the spine.

These findings comforted me as they did not point to a broken spine. Nevertheless, until I could be sure, I knew that I had to handle him as though his back were broken—always the safest course in such circumstances. A fractured vertebra does not cause serious damage unless the broken ends of the bones encroach or lacerate the spinal cord itself. One must assume from a history such as this that there is a possibility of a fractured spine, even though physical signs are lacking.

Stephen exhibited tenderness to pressure deep in his lower abdomen, and there was a questionable spasm of his stomach muscles, indicating the possibility of internal bleeding in the abdominal cavity. There was also tenderness over his rib cage on both sides. I could feel no obvious fractures of his pelvis.

His level of consciousness was puzzling. I could elicit a response only by being insistent, but otherwise he appeared to be "out of it." I wondered if there was an element of anxiety and perhaps hysteria involved. Jeremy drove slowly and carefully down the mountain track trying his best to cushion the bumps. Stephen moaned softly from time to time, and groaned as we passed over several large ruts. Two of the African firefighters rode in the back of the Land Rover, holding the bed board with Stephen firmly in place.

After what seemed an interminable trip, we arrived at the ranch airstrip. We then had to move Stephen into the plane while preserving his immobilization on the bed board. Jeremy took the two rear seats out of the Cessna. Measuring the dimensions of the bed board and comparing them to the floor of the plane confirmed our suspicion that the board was too large to fit. The tailgate of an old Land Rover also proved too large and bulky to use as a stretcher. Working carefully and in unison we managed to lift the bed board to the side of the open door of the plane and shift the blanket containing Stephen over onto the floor of the plane.

Twenty-five minutes later we landed at Nanyuki where we were met by the Caravan piloted by Trevor F. Jones. The emergency team, Dr. Alex Mula Mula and nurse Alex Gikani, fitted the spinal immobilization frame piece by piece to Stephen while he was still on the floor of Jeremy's plane. He was then moved to the larger plane, where an intravenous drip was started and oxygen administered.

The story had a happy ending. Stephen was flown to Wilson Airport where he was met by a Flying Doctors' ambulance and moved to the Nairobi Hospital. Over the next three days, while in intensive care, he was X-rayed and studied from head to toe, and found to have only non-serious bruises, truly a miracle after being run over by a tractor. Had he fallen under the rear wheels, which were heavily loaded with the weight of several firefighters, it is very likely that he would have been killed, or at least seriously injured.

The fire was fought during the remainder of the day and night. Nan and Carolyn filled fifty-gallon milk cans with hot tea, laced with milk and sugar. Many of the fighters had not eaten for over twenty-four hours, and many had drunk no water all day. I drove this much needed and welcome nutrition to the fire line. Many workers from surrounding ranches, and soldiers and policemen joined the fire-fighting line that night. The blaze was finally controlled, but not before many thousands of acres burned. The long rains were due any day, and promised a new and revitalized growth of grass and bush. Miraculously, none of the cattle or men were injured in the blaze. Thus ended our relaxing weekend of R & R at Jeremy's new ranch.

15

A Spy Among Us

By the end of the 1950s, the Cold War was in full force. Symbolically divided by the Berlin Wall, the Soviet bloc and the Western nations were vigorously competing for favor with the newly emerging countries of Africa and Asia, their attention fixed on the rich natural resources of these countries. They were also competing for the hearts and minds of the people. Africa was in turmoil. Countries were struggling for independence from colonial rule. The European powers, England, Germany, Portugal, France, Belgium and Spain had controlled the destinies of many African countries since Africa was mapped by European cartographers in the eighteenth century. The boundaries were decided by politics, often bearing little relation to tribal distribution or natural boundaries. The Belgian Congo, Mozambique and Angola, were in the throes of full-scale revolutions, with other countries about to follow. Determined to preserve their influence, the colonial powers struggled to maintain a large measure of control over the post-independence destiny of their colonies. Russia sought to introduce her brand of ideological colonialism to the emerging nations of Africa in her worldwide effort to spread communism. With the advent of "one country one vote" in the United Nations, the Soviets vigorously lobbied the new countries to join forces with the eastern bloc.

In this struggle, both Russia and the West (including the US) poured a never-ending stream of money and arms into Africa; a policy they subsequently came to regret when guns and money fueled revolution, clan warfare, religious war, genocide, and conquest in Somalia, the Sudan, Rwanda, the Belgian Congo, Uganda, Ethiopia, Angola, Mozambique, Liberia and Sierra Leone, devastating the economies and the peoples of these countries.

From the beginning, we in the Flying Doctors (AMREF) were determined never to mix in politics. Unwittingly, we became a pawn, albeit a small one, in the intelligence game being played throughout Africa at that crucial time in history.

From its inception, President John F. Kennedy forbade the Peace Corps to be a conduit for intelligence, espionage, or spying in any form. It was to remain pure in order to protect its credibility with the people of the countries that it served. The traditional techniques of gathering intelligence elsewhere in the world were of limited value or ineffective altogether in Africa. A Caucasian agent was conspicuous amongst dark-skinned populations. His physical contrast severely hampered his effectiveness, especially in countries where a diversity of tribes, clans, and religions mitigated against a commonality of language and traditions.

Embassy personnel stationed in Africa were understandably suspect. Their day-to-day activities were monitored closely. Placing operatives in the social or business structure and channeling money for intelligence purposes was difficult. With the sanctity of the Peace Corps inviolate, other avenues of laundering money to finance intelligence activities became imperative. Several NGOs (non-governmental organizations) operating in the Third World were recruited to serve as a conduit for both money and personnel during the 1950s and the 1960s. In some cases, these organizations were duped and used without the knowledge or permission of their governing bodies.

By 1960 the reputation of the Flying Doctors had spread throughout the rural areas of Kenya, Uganda, and Tanzania. There was considerable pressure to expand our resources already stretched to breaking point. The air fleet consisted of only two planes; the Piper Tripacer, and a twin-engine Aztec, the gift from Arthur Godfrey and "Pudge" Piper. To meet our increasing commitments, a full-time pilot was desperately needed; however, there was no place in the budget for a pilot's salary. As a consequence, the Aztec was underutilized and many needs unfulfilled.

As the saying goes, "out of the darkest moments often comes the sunshine." Early in 1960, James Monroe, a retired US Air Force Colonel and an active member of the original AMREF Board of Directors in the United States, called me one day with exciting news. Jim asked if I had ever heard of Mr. Allan James. I had heard of him and knew him to be a highly successful businessman with holdings in oil and retail stores, reputedly very wealthy.

Jim said that he had met one of Mr. James's top advisors at a social occasion and had filled him in on AMREF and the Flying Doctors of Africa. When their conversation was relayed to Mr. James, he was immediately interested, and expressed a desire to meet with me and discuss our project in Africa. Jim thought it might lead to obtaining some badly needed funds.

Of course, I was intrigued at the prospect, but then I had met influential people many times before in our never-ending quest for money. Rarely had it led to pay dirt.

An interview with Mr. James was arranged. He listened patiently for over an hour as I described the work of the Flying Doctors, and managed to emphasize our need for a pilot. He listened intently to my plea, interrupting me at intervals with relevant questions mostly relating to our operations in the bush, our radio network, the area we served, the local politics, our future plans, and so forth. He was non-committal when we parted but said he would explore ways that his non-profit foundation might help. I left the interview without great expectations but hoping, nevertheless, that I had made a conquest.

Several days later, Jim called with the good news that the Allan James Foundation was awarding us a grant to finance the costs of a pilot. I was delighted. I couldn't imagine why this important man would make such a generous grant after only one interview and without a great deal of red tape. I immediately telephoned Mike Wood in Nairobi with the good news. Needless to say, Mike was thrilled.

A few months later, Mr. Allan James was killed in a commercial plane crash. There was some mystery about his death. According to the newspapers, a large amount of cash was found on his body, but apparently there was no evidence of foul play. Nor were there any theories proposed as to why he was carrying such a large amount of money. The whole matter soon dropped from view.

As if by magic, Paul Morris, a pilot with extensive flying experience in many countries around the world, applied for the job and was promptly hired.

Paul was about forty-five at the time. He had seen action in China prior to the start of World War II. With the outbreak of war, Paul joined the Marine Air Corps, and fought his way through the Pacific and eventually Europe. Paul loved flying and was eager to fly for us in East Africa where he had never been. His wife and two daughters were veterans of overseas living, and they too looked forward to Nairobi, a beautiful small city where one could live very well and relatively inexpensively. Paul was a rare coin collector and skin-diver, which also accounted for his enthusiasm to work in Africa. It took him only about a month to pack up the family possessions and head for Kenya.

In February 1963, my overnight flight from London was met at Embakasi Airport in Nairobi by an uncharacteristically somber Michael Wood. His customary good cheer and welcoming exuberance were missing. I was puzzled by his mood. Things, I thought, had seemed to be going our way for a change. During the drive into town from the airport, he said very little except that we were going to an important meeting with a couple of men at the Norfolk Hotel where I was staying. He offered no further explanation except that the meeting concerned Flying Doctors' business.

After checking into the hotel, we went directly to my cottage. As soon as we were through the door, Michael wheeled, confronting me with a hurt look on his face. "Tom, why on earth did you guys in the US plant an intelligence agent in the Flying Doctors without talking to me first?"

I was completely taken aback. I had no idea what he was talking about, and I told him so. Mike said that he had discovered that Paul was an intelligence agent for the CIA, and reasoned that I must have known this when we hired him.

I was flabbergasted. Paul a spy? The idea never occurred to me. There was certainly nothing in Paul's history to arouse suspicion of such a past. His letters of recommendation had all been from responsible sources. Hindsight being twenty-twenty, it then dawned on me that Paul had appeared almost immediately after we had confirmation of a salary for a pilot from the James Foundation. I guess, had I thought about it, it would seem to be all too easy, too pat. But I still found it hard to believe that Paul was an intelligence agent.

About that moment, Mike answered a knock on the door and ushered two men into the room. Mike introduced them to me and identified them as British intelligence agents from MI6. I poured each of us a drink from the small bar, and we sat down for a chat.

For the better part of the next two hours I was grilled by the men about Paul. Where had he come from? Who had recommended him? Where did his salary come from? And many other questions about the details of his hiring. I answered as best I could, but of course I knew little that could be helpful.

"You see Dr. Rees, we know without any doubt that Paul is CIA. What we are somewhat puzzled about is why your government chose to place him here in Kenya with the Flying Doctors without doing us the courtesy of notifying us. After all, we are both on the same side, and it would seem useful to share information."

At this time, February 1963, Kenya was still a British Crown Colony and would remain so until she become independent in December of the same year; Kenya was thus still under the protection of the British Government. Since I was ignorant of these facts, it was not difficult to answer that I knew next to nothing of the whole affair. I suggested that they take it up with the US Government as the best source of information.

After the men had gone, I tried to convince Mike that I was as surprised by this news as he was. We talked for some time about what to do about Paul, if indeed the allegations were true. The last thing we wanted was to lose him if there was any way it could be avoided.

Later I learned that the CIA often used pilots in their surveillance of foreign countries. Pilots were mobile, they covered a lot of territory, were exposed to many people, and were sometimes able to be absent on trips for several days at a time without having to explain every minute of their whereabouts. Mike said that Paul had in fact been absent on a few occasions for two or three days at a time, ostensibly visiting Lamu and other old cities searching for rare old coins for his collection when he was technically off duty. These short trips had aroused curiosity, but not suspicion. Neither of us could come up with an answer as to why the British had not been informed if Paul was indeed working for United States intelligence; but then Kenya was just about to emerge as an independent nation and perhaps the United States wanted to cultivate its own sources of information.

I chose not to confront Paul with these allegations. Anyway, I was not sure how to play it. I decided to wait until I returned to New York to ferret out the details.

Paul was useful and very well-liked at the Flying Doctors, and was harming no one as far as we could see. Mike and I elected to leave things as they were for the time being. Clearly the problem would eventually have to be handled through government channels between the Brits and the US. Quite selfishly, we hated to lose the services of this excellent pilot and very nice man.

On my return to New York, I was able to confirm that Paul was indeed a career CIA pilot. Jim Monroe admitted that he had helped engineer the employment of Paul by the Flying Doctors and that the Allan James Foundation served as the conduit for his salary from the CIA. After Paul's cover was "blown" to the British, we later learned that the CIA and MI6 had got together and were sharing the intelligence information provided by Paul. During his tenure of three years with the Flying Doctors, Africa was a political hotbed. Paul made several flights into "hot" areas of activity, especially the Congo. A further need of US intelligence in the East African area was dictated by the space program which at the time was planning the first moon landing. Appropriate relay, communications, and rescue stations around the globe relating to space travel were being investigated. High mountains such as Kilimanjaro and Mount Kenya became important in the plans.

Paul and his family retired to Portugal in 1964 to pursue his hobbies of coin collecting and sailing. His role as an intelligence agent was known only to Michael, myself, Jim Monroe, and the intelligence communities of Britain and the US. His role as an employee of the CIA did not become common knowledge at AMREF headquarters. It was unlikely that anyone had suspected this mild-mannered and likable man piloting the Aztec on many medical missions was, in fact, a "spy."

Towards the end of the 1960s, newspapers reported that a number of non-profit foundations were sheltering intelligence activities. There was an outcry from Congress and from the public forcing discontinuance of the practice.

16

The Making of a Surgeon

Almost from my earliest memory, I dreamed of becoming a doctor. This goal was so deeply ingrained in my early life that I never really considered any other career. The medical exploits of my doctor uncles were regular bedtime stories for me. I remember one in particular.

Two of my uncles were the only doctors in a rural valley in Afton, Wyoming. Before modern roads and snow-removal equipment, this valley was inaccessible for several weeks each winter when both of the passes that provided access to it were closed by deep snow. In 1914 a devastating worldwide flu epidemic struck, and the Ruby Valley of Wyoming did not escape. Soon, all of the beds of the small hospital in Afton were full with the sick and the dead. The corridors were filled with patients on the floor when beds were no longer available. The snow outside the hospital was four feet deep and when a patient died, the only recourse was to place the body outside in the snow since digging graves was out of the question. Those who died on the second floor of the hospital were literally pushed out of the window onto the snow-covered ground where they awaited proper burial when the snow melted and manpower was available to dig graves. In the midst of the epidemic, one of my uncles contracted the disease and died. The remaining brother found it necessary to drop his brother's body out of the window and leave him in the snow until later when he could be properly prepared for burial. I heard this ghastly, but heroic (in my eyes) story of the hard work and sacrifices of my uncles over and over again. I considered them to be true heroes and this only whetted my appetite for becoming a doctor even more.

I imagine that the first words whispered into my newborn ear while snuggling in my mother's arms were something like "Here's my little doctor." To my mother, a medical career spelled prestige and security. My father's family regarded medicine as the most honorable profession, the ultimate fulfilling career, and in keeping with the family's Mormon tradition, a very real way to help people. I am sure that attitude was conveyed to me at an early age.

Although my father's three brothers were all medical doctors, he did not choose a medical career for himself, but became fascinated with the study of biology while in pre-medicine. He had a long and distinguished career as Chairman of the Department of Life Sciences at the University of Utah. There are over twenty-six medical practitioners in my extended family, all stemming, I am sure, from my paternal grandmother's determination.

Mother's family were farmers in the beautiful Sanpete Valley of central Utah. Her grandparents were converted to the Mormon Church in Denmark and followed Brigham Young in a wagon train in 1856 in the great emigration to Utah to be part of the new Mormon kingdom in the West. They scratched a meager living farming grain, alfalfa and peas out of the rocky soil, as well as raising a few head of livestock. Family life was interrupted at intervals by the Mormon Church calling upon mother's father to go abroad as a missionary. These missions lasted two years at a time, and the expenses were born entirely by the family. While serving the church, these extended trips abroad were financially devastating to the family at home. My grandmother somehow managed to eke out an existence from the small farm, which was minimally productive at best.

My mother never forgot those years of struggle. The memories of going without was deeply ingrained in her. She was determined that such a state of near poverty would not prevail in her own family. Her childhood hardships fueled her fierce determination that her own children must become financially successful at all costs. By a succession of menial jobs, she managed to obtain a junior college education, and after marriage to my father she became a skilled executive secretary. My brother and I owe much of our continuing drive to become doctors to mother's unwavering dedication to that goal.

My father's family were also Mormon pioneers. They emigrated to America from Wales to seek a new life in the "promised land" envisioned by Brigham Young in the Great Salt Lake Valley of Utah where, as Mormons, they could live in peace. Unable to afford a Conestoga wagon and a team of horses or oxen, my paternal grandfather's family pushed a handcart with the Bunker Mormon handcart company in 1856 across the Great Plains from Winter Quarters near Council Bluffs, Iowa, to Salt Lake City,

Utah—a distance of some one thousand miles, and a feat almost incomprehensible to the present generation.

My paternal grandmother crossed the plains in a covered wagon at the age of eight with her father and two sisters in 1869. Her mother had died of childbirth fever the year before. There were incredible hardships and many deaths along the way. Bodies were simply buried on the trail where they fell. Life was hard and the sacrifices were staggering. Both families of my paternal grandmother and grandfather had been coal miners in Wales, accordingly they were sent by Brigham Young to the Sanpete Valley of central Utah because a vein of coal was found there. Unfortunately, this small coal vein soon petered out. Of necessity, they raised cattle and sheep on small ranches that they homesteaded. Alfalfa and wild hay were raised in the summer for winter feed. They grazed the livestock in the mountains during the summer months.

My father was one of nine children. From infancy the children were indoctrinated with the virtues of higher education. As a small child I remember well my grandmother's continuous lectures on the values of education. She believed all men should be doctors and all women teachers. She had no intention of seeing her nine children struggle to scratch a hard living on a small ranch as she and my grandfather had done. Her relentless lobbying managed to see all nine through university. Three of the sons became medical doctors and the fourth, my father, a university professor. The daughters were educated as school teachers—medicine was not an option for women in those days. My paternal grandfather also served overseas as a missionary for the Church as did two of his sons (including my father). He was called to mission work almost immediately after his marriage. His young bride remained behind to farm the ranch. Times were tough but the people were strong.

With such an emphasis on medicine as a career it is not difficult to understand why I was started on the road to a medical career at a very early age. It seemed inconceivable that I could do anything else and so I followed a straight path to a medical degree with only one detour. Thank God I loved medicine, for I was never prepared for any other life.

The detour was my infatuation with jazz music. I fell in love with the saxophone the first time I heard one while listening to a young band at a school dance when I was about ten. That led to an intense love affair with jazz that persists to this day. I studied saxophone and clarinet and played in the school band. I saved every spare cent I could get my hands on to buy records. I copied the saxophone solos of Johnny Hodges, Willy

Smith, Lester Young, Benny Carter, Coleman Hawkins, and other great reed players of the day. The constant racket from my room almost drove my parents mad.

Along with several other youngsters of about my age (twelve) who shared my infatuation with jazz and were studying various instruments, we formed a jazz band. It was during the height of the "swing era" in the early forties. We worshiped Benny Goodman, Tommy Dorsey, Artie Shaw, Charlie Barnet, Duke Ellington, Jimmy Lunceford, Count Basie, and the many other bands of the day. Whenever one of these big bands came to town we managed to hear them (underage as we were)—lapping up every note played.

I loved playing jazz. Our small band stayed together and grew to an impressive eighteen-piece orchestra by the time I was fifteen. We played all the local proms, church dances, private clubs and finally became the relief house band at the premier dance hall in Salt Lake where we filled in between the appearances of many traveling big-name swing bands.

For a brief moment, I became serious about jazz music as a career but I knew that it would alienate my family. I loved to play. I enjoyed the camaraderie of my fellow musicians. I admired their lack of prejudice and their warm support for each other. Musicians are a close-knit fraternity. For a while, I toyed with the idea of becoming a professional musician.

Often during World War II traveling bands arrived in Salt Lake minus one or more sidemen because of the draft and the rapid turnover of jazz personnel in those days. The guys in our band and I were often called on by the musician's union to fill the vacant chairs during a band's stay in Salt Lake. In this way, much to my intense joy, I filled in as a temporary sax player in the bands of Fletcher Henderson, Woody Herman, and Stan Kenton. Those were some of the most thrilling experiences of my lifetime. They are as vivid in my memory now as they were over a half century ago. I also learned how grueling life on the road was. I was turned off by the cavalier attitude too many musicians had about drugs. I was not a prude. Smoking pot on the job was one thing, but the use of "hard" drugs such as morphine, heroin or cocaine was quite another matter. I was appalled at the use of drugs, often by the top musicians, in the band business, but the final consideration that turned me away from a career in music was the realization that my true love was medicine.

My father threatened that if my grades in university slipped from As or Bs, he would no longer tolerate my playing jazz gigs. I really burned the midnight oil to get the marks and keep playing. Of course, after I entered medical school my night playing was severely limited anyway.

Despite the lofty opinions held by my mother and father, I was not idealistic about a medical career. I followed the career path more or less because it was expected of me, but as time went on, I found medicine more and more appealing. I could see from the example of my uncles that being a doctor brought prestige, a comfortable living and security. In addition, it seemed an excellent way to be independent and free from the dictates of others. I was also attracted to medicine as a good way to help people. It was not until I became involved in Africa that medicine took on a whole new meaning for me. It was through my experiences there that the spiritual side of being a doctor surfaced.

After graduating from the University of Utah Medical School I began a training in surgery that lasted for seven years before becoming a fully-fledged plastic surgeon. The first five years of internship and residency were in general surgery, a prerequisite for plastic surgery, followed by two years of plastic surgery, and after that, one year of fellowship in England. My training included stints in Rochester, New York, a brief time at Yale, and the remainder of my training at the prestigious New York Hospital-Cornell Medical Center in New York City.

During my initial years of training in general surgery, I discovered a specialty that fulfilled my needs—plastic surgery. I found plastic surgery to be a real challenge, one that offered an opportunity to be innovative and constructive. Repairing physical deformities is not only technically difficult, but spiritually rewarding for both surgeon and patient. Sometimes it can be almost a miracle for a patient who has suffered a loss of self-image and confidence through a cruel trick of nature or an accident. Plastic surgery suited me perfectly.

My plastic surgery training in New York was under the tutelage of a brilliant but authoritarian chief—Dr. Herbert Conway. It was then that I had the opportunity of topping off my formal training with the Mark's Fellowship under Sir Archibald McIndoe. The repair of the burned RAF pilots was still under way ten years after the War and I had the opportunity to help with some of those patients as well as enjoy the opportunity to learn the full spectrum of day-to-day plastic surgery.

Despite the demands on one's health and psyche, for me, surgical residency was an intensely rewarding experience, a fulfilling period of learning probably never to be equaled again in my lifetime. I knew, at graduation, that I would never again be so knowledgeable no matter how hard I tried to keep up.

The constant challenge of learning, and the growing responsibility for taking care of sick and injured people was intensely stimulating. I also enjoyed the strong bonds of friendships formed with fellow residents, many of which persist to this day.

Chronic sleep deprivation was very difficult for me. I worried about the possible long-term consequences on my health and about making mistakes. Many of the menial and time-consuming tasks (now done by technicians) assigned to residents in the 1950s reflected the belief that a Spartan existence was good for us. A work day of eighteen to twenty hours was not unusual for a resident or intern. Today, legislation has somewhat shortened these killing hours, but not much. We worked such sadistic hours because it was expected of us. The hospitals benefited from our cheap labor.

Before World War II, marriage was considered to be a distraction, forbidden in most surgical training programs. The extra-hospital demands imposed by marriage were thought to impair the residents' efficiency. It was thought that every quantum of energy was required to do the job leaving none over for the duties of marriage. World War II changed all of that. After 1945, many residents were veterans; older, more experienced, and often married. Actually, married residents proved more dependable and stable than their single peers.

Money was a problem for a married resident couple. The meager stipend paid by many major institutions did not suffice. We subsisted through those difficult years largely through the efforts of my wife Nan. Her education at Bennington College in Vermont and the Art Students League in New York focused on art, but did not equip her to earn money. She was well aware of the problems we faced when we decided to marry while I was an intern.

We fell in love and decided to marry despite our families' admonitions to wait. We simply could not imagine waiting all those years until I completed residency training. In those days a surgical intern earned $100 per month in top university teaching hospitals. Residents were paid a little more with each successive year. The hospital also provided laundry of our white uniforms, and food (provided we ate in the hospital cafeteria). A room was also provided at the hospital, but spouses were not allowed. No provision was made for living "off base." We knew that somehow we would survive it all—love would triumph.

Nan's parents considered me to be a cowboy from out West and disapproved (not strenuously) of her marrying me. Nevertheless, I summoned all my courage and in the best traditions of a conservative Eastern family, asked her father for her hand in marriage. Before answering, he told me that despite her education she was in no position to make money.

"How much money do you earn young man?" "About one-hundred dollars a month, Sir." "That will not even keep her in cigarettes [we all smoked in those days]. How do you propose to support her?" "I am sure she can find some work, Sir. We can live frugally."

We married and set up housekeeping in New York City. Nan went out to look for work, trudging the streets of New York. Her art degree from Bennington did not make her especially employable in a market place demanding clerical skills. Nan couldn't even type. Fortunately, Nan was gifted with great beauty and charm. A friend arranged an interview with Eileen Ford who had recently started a model agency in New York which became the premier agency in the world. Nan showed up one day while she was on the telephone. Eileen motioned her to come in and while she continued her phone conversation, said to the person on the other end of the phone, "I have someone here that might suit you." She hung up, gave Nan an address and told her to take her portfolio with her. Nan didn't have a portfolio, so she went back to our apartment, picked up our wedding album and headed out.

The sophisticated editors of *Glamour* magazine were highly amused when Nan showed up with her wedding pictures, but hired her on the spot nevertheless. Her first assignment was a cover on *Glamour*. Covers on *Mademoiselle*, *Vogue*, and other fashion magazines followed, and Nan's career was launched. When television began to establish itself as a popular medium in the late 1940s and 1950s, Nan appeared as a commercial spokesperson and appeared on the *Today Show* with Dave Garroway and the *Tonight Show* with Jack Paar, amongst others. These experiences proved most helpful as a background for her role in organizing celebrity events that helped raise funds for the struggling Flying Doctors. Among the events were several Safari Balls for prominent New Yorkers and a black-tie Carnegie Hall concert featuring Miles Davis and the Gil Evans Orchestra. This was Miles's first concert at Carnegie Hall and raised enough money for us to run the Flying Doctors for nearly two years. Nan supported us quite handsomely. After fifty years of marriage, she has lost none of her beauty or her charm.

When I completed my residency in New York, we took our meager savings and headed for Europe. Our plan was to see Europe before we settled down to build a practice in New York City. We figured that once I opened an office, it would be a long time before we could afford either the time or money to take such a trip. Also, I was keen to visit the European plastic surgery units made famous by World War II, and the well-known surgeons who directed them. I wanted to expand my knowledge of my chosen specialty. It was during this trip that I visited East Grinstead to observe the great McIndoe at work. It was there that the string of events began that culminated in the formation of the Flying Doctors of East Africa.

I was fascinated watching the great surgeon at work. His surgical list each day was prodigious, and he graciously explained each and every surgical problem to me and then showed me how to solve it. After a few days observing him, to our astonishment, Nan and I were invited to have dinner with McIndoe and his wife Connie. It was one of those rare meetings in life where everyone clicked. The chemistry was positive all around, including Connie and Nan who instantly hit it off. During this visit to his clinic, Sir Archibald offered me a fellowship.

"You are lucky," he said, "There is an unexpected sudden vacancy of the Mark's Fellowship which has been occupied by Michael Wood, a surgeon from Kenya who must return home for family reasons. Would you like to have this position for a few months?"

Of course I accepted his offer instantly. I do not think he offered me the job because he thought I was an extraordinary surgeon of great promise. It was a combination of things, not the least of which was our instant warm personal bonding. Was this a fortuitous happening or fate? I believe it to be the beginning of a pattern that led to the Flying Doctors and the thousands of people that have been helped by them.

Shortly after finishing my fellowship in England, I returned to New York to begin my career, only to be recalled to active duty by the US Navy for two years. However, it was a rewarding time, richly expanding my surgical experience as Chief of Plastic Surgery at the St. Albans Naval Hospital in the suburbs of New York City. This second tour of Naval duty was a pay-back for six months of active duty as a hospital corpsman in the US Navy in 1945.

Finally, in 1958, I was discharged from the US Navy and ready to start my career in New York City, the most competitive city in the world. As the song goes, "If you can make it here, you can make it anywhere"—such was the compelling draw of this exciting city with its long-established medical traditions of the great surgeons of the day who, in addition to their private practices, were also the respected and famous teachers in the great hospitals of the city. One thing was crystal clear to me—there was only one way to go in New York City and that was to the top. Becoming just another surgeon in this huge city did not appeal to me. The question was, how to get there? How does one put oneself forward? Advertising in those days was considered disreputable and anyway, spelled professional suicide. The Supreme Court had not yet decided that advertising by professionals was not illegal.

The only road to success was hard work, seizing every advantage, cultivating many friends and acquaintances and, hopefully, a stroke of luck. My New Zealand-born mentor, Sir Archibald, told me over and over again, "Tom, all you have to do is to operate successfully on that first one thousand patients, and from then on your career is assured." Of course, what he also meant, but did not articulate, was that it was extremely helpful if at least one or two of this first thousand were important, high-profile individuals who would praise my skill far and wide. McIndoe knew, for he counted amongst his practice the most famous people of the post-World War II era.

Four years of undergraduate university, four years of medical school, followed by seven years of progressive surgical training through internship, residency and fellowship, then a second hitch in the US Navy were all under my belt. I was ready to go, and because of my introduction to Africa, I had an additional compelling interest in medicine. I was undoubtedly at my peak; saturated with knowledge and training. Nevertheless, I lacked experience which, along with wisdom and expertise, would come with time.

Patients have no foolproof way of evaluating the skill of a surgeon (except through hearsay), but do respond to a positive attitude and the ability of the surgeon to communicate with them. They are greatly influenced by their "gut reaction" to a doctor. A surgeon can be a master in the operating room, but if he or she cannot project confidence, many patients will go elsewhere. It has been said that A students make the best academicians, B students make the best doctors, and the C students make the most money. There may be some truth in that statement. C students are apt to have more communicative skills—the best "bedside manner."

I believe that the success of a treatment depends a good deal on a positive relationship between doctor and patient, a theory strongly supported during my years of travel in Africa. The traditional doctor or "witch doctor," through positive reinforcement of his treatment, has a strong influence on patients. It is well known that in some tribes, the traditional doctor can will a patient's demise with no apparent scientific explanation. Alternative medicine has a salutary effect on many patients because they believe it will help. Acupuncture, herbal therapy, mushroom juice, or St. John's Wort will help if the patient *believes* in the practitioner.

Often it is simply a matter of chemistry between doctor and patient. I have always been leery of treating a patient whom I felt reacted negatively to my personality.

In fact, during my later years of surgical practice, I declined to treat patients with whom I could not feel a positive communication—"good chemistry." I can look back on several unpleasant experiences with patients during my career that, in most cases, could have been avoided had I listened to that inner voice during the initial consultation that told me, "Look out, there's something wrong here."

I knew from the beginning that I wanted to be a skilled surgeon, a very successful practitioner with a top-flight private practice, and a teacher. I wanted to be respected by my peers in academia. I wanted it all. I tried diligently to learn the not-so-easy-to-teach techniques of successful communication with patients; how to instill confidence; how to let the patient understand that *I really was concerned about them*; and the ability to heal them. In current terms of reference, I suppose the doctors with the best bedside manners possess "emotional intelligence" as well as cognitive knowledge. I suspect the knack of interacting effortlessly with other humans is largely an inborn trait; however, much can be learned by the willing student from those who are masters at it. Unfortunately, in our modern world of HMOs (health maintenance organizations), group practice, institutional medicine, and corporate medicine, the old-fashioned bedside manner is not emphasized. When I finished surgical training in 1956 private practitioners were in healthy competition for patients. A polished bedside manner was certainly as essential as medical skill.

I quickly learned that being thoroughly trained with all of the right degrees and postgraduate "tickets" as well as references was not sufficient to gain either hospital privileges or career advancement in New York City. I thought that the years of training in a major institution like New York Hospital and my fellowship in England as well as the rewarding time in the Navy as the surgeon in charge of a large department in a Naval Hospital, eminently qualified me for a hospital appointment in a city the size of New York. How naive I was. I ran smack into medical politics in the real world for the first time. In 1958, there were really only a dozen or so plastic surgeons in New York City. This handful of men (no woman) controlled the hospital appointments in plastic surgery in virtually all of the hospitals. A closed-door policy was strongly enforced.

I visited each of these "chiefs," pleading for a hospital appointment. I was told by each that there was simply no room in New York, not enough patients to go around, and that I should probably look at California or Florida as a more likely place to practice. It is hard to imagine now that a few surgeons were able to control the accessibility to plastic surgery in a city with a population the size of New York's. This dozen or so men exercised a headlock on hospital appointments and were able to freeze out young surgeons such as myself. I was shocked and outraged, but the system had been in existence for a long time and seemed impenetrable. The only access was by becoming an assistant to one of these medical moguls and gradually worming one's way into the system; however, such positions were few and far between.

I was discouraged with this news, but these refusals only strengthened my resolve to practice where I pleased—in New York City. I faced a very tough task. After about seven years in and around New York, Nan and I had met a fair number of people through her work and mine. I also knew quite a few doctors, but the only ones that would be likely to refer patients to me as a young man just out of training were peers, equally young and without practices of their own. The older, established physicians had set up referral ties to physicians in their own age group and were unlikely to refer to young men.

After much effort, I finally managed to obtain a staff appointment to Doctors Hospital, a prestigious private hospital where I could take my private patients (when I had any). I yearned for an appointment at a bona fide teaching hospital. I really did not like the idea of being only a private practitioner. Finally, I obtained an appointment on the faculty of New York Postgraduate University at Bellevue Hospital, overcoming the objection of the plastic surgeon in charge of the service. At least now I had an opportunity to launch my career. My father often told me that success in life frequently arose through opportunity, but that preparation was the key to turning opportunity into a true success. I was well-trained, I was confident of my skills as a surgeon and in my personal relationships. All I had to do was work hard, be confident, and keep my eyes on the goal.

I found a minuscule office on 72nd Street and Madison Avenue—not Park Avenue, but in the very acceptable "East Side" area for professional offices. We furnished it with cheap but attractive furniture salvaged from Nan's parents' attic and a modern Swedish store. Archie McIndoe once told me that a surgeon's office need not be fancy, but it should be as comfortable for a taxi driver's wife as for a Vanderbilt. We thought this one was. Now all I needed were patients, and they came in due course.

So many people I know, sharing their innermost thoughts during a personal moment, admit that there is something missing in their lives—a sort of hole in the consciousness; a vague awareness of being incomplete; a yearning that they cannot articulate. No matter how successful, busy, famous, or powerful they may be, they sense that somewhere, somehow, an unrealized need exists in their lives. Our world is complex and confusing; more so than in any previous time in history: survival is difficult enough, let alone finding spiritual satisfaction. Attaining inner fulfillment seems always just beyond one's grasp. The wealthy give money and support worthwhile causes in an attempt to fill this gap. The accumulation of wealth, power and "things" does not bring inner peace. In my experience only service to others brings real inner satisfaction.

I have been fortunate enough to know many who have devoted their lives to serving others, and I am in awe of such people, who project an aura of serenity and completeness. In an age of confusion they seem to know who they are. Serving in non-profit humanitarian organizations such as the Peace Corps, CARE, Oxfam, Save the Children Fund, UNICEF, African Medical and Research Foundation, Doctors Without Borders, Doctor to the World, and many others, often provides the stimulus that starts many young people on a career path of service to humanity. Many young people working in such programs become addicted to the sense of fulfillment and inner joy that their work provides. They are able to identify a goal early in life.

In the more developed nations, the struggle for basic survival—shelter, food, protective clothing, and procreation—is complicated by the additional struggle for "success." In Africa, as in all Third World countries, there is little chance for a person to escape beyond the environment into which they have been born. There is still only a remote possibility of achieving substantial material comfort, or what we in the West consider to be success.

The spiritual mystery of Africa intrigued me during my first visit to that land. I experienced a bonding to the countries and their people, and on each succeeding visit, that bond was strengthened. After each trip, I returned to the highly sophisticated world of New York City struggling with my conscience and searching my soul to justify my work in this "civilized" society where, by now, there seemed to be a plastic surgeon on every corner. I actually felt even deprived, cheated to have left so many patients behind me in Africa who desperately needed my skill. Sometimes I felt ashamed that my work in New York seemed so inconsequential, while in Africa I knew that I was making a real difference no matter how small. Most of my patients in New York sought plastic surgery to improve their appearance for a variety of reasons, not the least of which was to conform to the concepts of physical beauty dictated by TV, motion pictures, or magazines.

For years I considered my work in New York as unimportant. I now know that this was unfair to my patients. Suffering cannot be defined by boundaries. A teenager with a large nose or huge breasts bears emotional scars as does a patient with a cleft lip. Suffering is not quantitative. Each person suffers in his own way. A minor physical problem for one person can be an overwhelming one for someone else. Plastic surgeons and psychologists know that self-image is a complex area in human psychology. A person's self-image may bear no relationship to the reality as perceived by others. Self-adornment and self-mutilation are popular methods of enhancing beauty in some societies. Thus, ancient tribal customs of scarification and tattooing are unacceptable in most modern societies, but are the norm in many tribes. Primitive man incises, scarifies, paints, and decorates himself as an acceptable expression of ego manifestation, while modern "civilized" man indulges in lesser degrees of self-adornment. "Excessive" examples of self-beautification (or self-mutilation) are thought to represent inner feelings of frustration, hostility, or aggression.

In recent years the young have adopted traditional ancient methods of self-adornment. Various ornaments such as shells, wooden plugs and stakes, precious and semiprecious stones, and metals are inserted into perforations of the nose, ears, cheeks, lips, tongue, and genitalia. Stretching the lower lip (Ubangi style), or the genitalia—common practices in some African tribes and South Pacific cultures—has not yet come into vogue in the West. However, plumping the lips up with collagen or silicone injections is considered sexy. In pre-Columbian culture, persons with congenital deformities such as harelip, dwarfism, and spinal deformities (hunchback) were revered and even accorded special privileges by society.

The inevitable physical signs of aging can be devastating, especially to women. The fact is, attractive and younger-looking women are more successful in finding both a mate and a good job. The divorced or widowed middle-aged woman is at a disadvantage from every point of view. Middle-aged men are more apt to be passed over for promotion to top executive positions which are awarded instead to those who look younger (and therefore more vigorous). I eventually realized that moderating the aging process through surgery is not a trivial or frivolous pursuit.

Epilogue

Now that I am retired from the day-to-day responsibilities of an active surgical practice, I can reflect on what I have learned from more than forty years of involvement with medicine in Africa. One message that rings out loud and clear: whether we like it or not, we are our brother's keeper. The developed world of the West has necessarily, if reluctantly, entered into a partnership with the developing world of Africa. Our age of instant communication and rapid transportation has forged a social, economic and medical interdependency of these two worlds. No country or continent can live in isolation ever again, especially where disease is concerned. Disease knows no boundaries.

Unfortunately, it is true that the average person in America or Europe knows little about the people of the developing world, except in times of strife or human calamity. In recent years the media has graphically reported wars, genocide, famine, military coups, epidemics and other human abominations in the Sudan, Somalia, Rwanda, the Congo, Sierra Leone, Liberia, Uganda, South Africa and elsewhere. However, an all too common reaction is "Thank God, it's them and not us." I have so often heard people remark that it is the "primitive culture" of indigenous Africans that explains the repeated tragedies reported in the media. But this is a bigoted argument that fails in the face of reality.

Our modern world is not static, especially in the developing countries where social and political changes are often abrupt and rarely follow predications, and where surprises are the rule rather than the exception. While medical care is generally recognized as being of the utmost importance to national development ("A healthy people are a productive people"), in virtually every African country a paltry portion of the national budget is allotted to medical services. Funds for medical care are given low priority, lagging behind defense, agriculture, commerce and education in the budgets of most African countries. This prioritization is upside down, since without a healthy population, general development of a society is seriously impeded.

Important sources of funds in developing countries, such as the World Bank and the International Monetary Fund may recognize that a healthy society is a necessity, yet health care funding, until very recently, has not occupied an important place on their agendas. Hopefully, there are significant indications that this attitude is changing. Most African countries operate on a health care budget of three to five dollars per capita per year, compared to several hundred dollars in Europe and America. Emergencies such as epidemics and armed conflicts often deplete these allocations, leaving funds for preventative medicine in short supply. In the competition for budgetary allocations, medical care inevitably gives way to social and political pressures. And where corruption is prevalent, as it is virtually everywhere, funds that should go for medical services are plundered.

In addition to insufficient funding, health care in Africa suffers from lack of interest. Educated medical providers are slowly increasing in numbers in most African countries. But African doctors, nurses, technicians and paramedics suffer from the same problems as graduates of higher education in any field; there are not enough salaried positions to support them, even when the need is great and jobs are available. Many positions in the rural areas go unfilled because of the reluctance of trained professionals to seek a career away from cities and towns.

In health care, as in all else, money talks. We get what we pay for. Where money is available and treatment exists, rapid and substantial progress can be made in the fight against disease. All too often in the developing world, treatment is unavailable simply because it is too expensive.

AIDS is a case in point. AIDS is no longer necessarily a death sentence in the developed world, as it once was. The newer drug "cocktail" combinations apparently arrest or prolong progression of the disease. Unfortunately, in Africa the cost of such treatment is almost prohibitive. Despite its status as the worldwide medical scourge of our time, AIDS has become an economic disease—treatable in those who have, and not treatable in those who have not. AIDS, like the plague of the Middle Ages, is decimating many parts of Africa and Asia, where it is lethal for most patients, simply because treatment is unaffordable and educational efforts at prevention are poorly supported.

The World Health Organization predicts that in some countries such as Zambia, Botswana and Zimbabwe, entire generations may perish from AIDS in the next ten years and that the average length of life will decline from sixty to forty—a horrendous step backward. In many areas of Africa the HIV rate is thirty percent and rising. In Zimbabwe, for example, two hundred people die every day of AIDS—73,000 each year. Yet in other countries such as Uganda, where sex and AIDS education has been promoted by the government and accepted by the people, the incidence is declining.

The gap between the developed world and the developing world grows ever wider and economic discrimination against those affected in the Third World increases. Denial, discrimination and ignorance also mitigate against control of sexually-transmitted diseases such as AIDS. People who are positive for HIV are commonly isolated and discriminated against in many countries in Africa. Recently in South Africa a woman was beaten and stoned to death by her neighbors for trying to convince those who were HIV-positive to come forward and be treated.

Many treatment and HIV care centers in African countries are vacant, yet people are dying everywhere, isolated from their families and society. HIV-positive women are persecuted and often expelled from the family by their husbands. Both men and women can lose their jobs if it becomes known that they are HIV-positive. Some mines in South Africa hire four people for every job, reasoning that three of the four will be dead in a short while.

Fighting this grim scenario is a cadre of health care professionals who are dedicated to improving the medical lot of the people of the Third World. These professionals, both African and expatriate, forego lucrative and otherwise rewarding careers, to devote their energies and talents to the developing world. Despite civil wars, epidemics, famine and political disruption, their commitment to humankind is real and does not falter.

Eventually Africa and Africans will solve their own problems, but only with temporary help and direction from the developed world. Self-reliance is the only viable long-term answer that makes sense. For the time being, infusions of money and medical talent must continue, and attempts to change behavior must keep pace with the delivery of health care to achieve the goal of self-reliance. The apparent snail's pace at which these changes occur is frustrating, but change does not come about through declaration, only through evolution.

Even a "super specialty" such as plastic surgery has much to contribute. Diseases such as malaria, diarrhea, tuberculosis, AIDS and others are rampant and need urgent care—but so does disfigurement. Physical deformities are regarded with fear and sometimes awe in all societies. As we have seen in some areas of East Africa, persons deformed by the ravages of leprosy are outcast from their families and homes. People with birth deformities, such as cleft lip and other defects, often end up begging for a living. Even in our most enlightened societies, the "ugly" person is handicapped in seeking employment and social acceptance, subtle as such discrimination might be. The ability to correct deformity and thereby heal the afflicted soul is as necessary in Africa as it is anywhere.

Opportunities for advance seem to be shrinking for many people. Greed and corruption permeates every aspect of life, both in government and the private sector. "Kleptocracy" is a newly-coined word to describe many African governments riddled with corruption. Corruption is so widespread that it has become the norm in many African countries, impeding social and economic advances in every way. Increasingly discouraged and feeling impotent, educated young professionals are deeply concerned for the future of themselves and their countries.

Only by understanding the reality of our bond with the developing world, and the necessity of long-term commitment to help our less fortunate neighbors, can we make a lasting difference—and then only by promoting self-reliance. We are a long way from assuming that kind of collective responsibility and commitment. Those in power who control the African countries likewise have a responsibility. Change cannot be entirely the responsibility of outsiders. Graft and corruption can only be controlled by accountability, and the provision of effective leadership dedicated to making the changes required to achieve real progress.

I am in awe of those special people who devote their lives to helping others. During the last forty-odd years I have met many who have done so: doctors, nurses, health workers, missionaries, Peace Corps workers, those who work for foundations and non-governmental organizations and others. While somewhat skeptical at first about their motivations, after working with these professionals for all these years, I now sincerely believe that it is a labor of love. After spending a lifetime working under difficult conditions, many have little to show for it at the end. Meager retirement benefits, if any, and often no health plan to see them through old age. These are basics that most of us consider a rightful reward.

I believe that simple differences in perception and communication are the basis for so many problems and misunderstandings between the developed and the developing world. The problem is one of communication and patterns of behavior. In the mistaken belief that behavior can be changed by words only, we in the developed world expect to change the behavior and cultural attitudes of other people to conform to what we perceive as acceptable standards simply by telling them how they should live. It is not hard to understand that peoples of the Third World stubbornly cling to their traditional ways. They want to protect themselves from what they perceive as an outside threat to their way of life.

Attempts at birth control (the politically correct term is "population containment") by the conventional means of Western-style education is an example of how the best of intentions can result in failure. The concept of family planning is in direct conflict with traditional behavior in many tribes where sexual promiscuity is the norm. The goal of many African men is to have as many children as possible, thus insuring comfort and security in their old age. Consequently, many birth control efforts in developing countries have failed miserably. Kenya, for example (until the current AIDS epidemic), was experiencing a four percent per annum increase in the population, thus doubling the population roughly every twenty-five years. Similar figures exist for many other developing countries all over the world. Available food and water supplies are already marginal in many places and will not be able to support such an increase in population in the future.

Likewise, as we have seen, female genital mutilation (circumcision), a ghastly custom, is hard to abolish in some societies, for without it there is little chance of a young woman obtaining a husband. Practically, the behavioral changes necessary to change this tradition are complicated and difficult despite what "outsiders" think. The sexual act is of prime importance in most countries of the developing world, more so than in the West. It is the principal form of recreation where there is no cinema or TV to occupy what leisure time is available. Any teaching that seeks to limit sex is hard to sell. Condoms, withdrawal, or other methods of sexual interruption are anathema to many men, and female contraceptives are often complicated and expensive for women. Characteristically, attempts by women to initiate any form of contraception is often met with stubborn resistance by the men.

Promiscuity, or at least what we regard to be promiscuity, is not regarded as a sin, but as normal behavior by many tribes in rural Africa. Nomads especially tend to be promiscuous. Sexual promiscuity is common among many nomadic workers such as truck drivers, fishermen and miners. Some such nomadic workers have several wives, one at home, and another one or two along the way. In pastoral nomadic tribes such as the Maasai a male has access to a considerable number of women who are married to his circumcision brothers; sometimes over a thousand women.

Promiscuity probably once made sense for wandering herders, but now it is the principal means of spreading sexually transmitted infections and diseases. Women, except those who are educated and urbanized, still have little or nothing to say about sexual practices. Women in Africa are just beginning to protest their limited role in society and are clamoring for equal rights; however, male chauvinism is still the order of the day.

There has been a progressive and rapidly accelerating destruction of the chief economic asset of East Africa—wild game. The tourist business is basically what keeps Kenya afloat, and could do the same quite easily for Tanzania as well. It is the tourist dollar that counts for the economy of Kenya. Coffee, tea, and other exports could in no way approach balancing the budget, since generation after generation of political leaders have corrupted the system or turned a blind eye to the steady game decimation that goes on. The money from overseas exportation of the products of wild animals, especially elephant tusks and rhinoceros horn, finds its way into all sorts of pockets, all too often those of government officials who may be graduates of universities.

Half-hearted lip service is often given to the need to control the poaching of these animals, yet the resources made available to stop poaching or to punish those who promote it are meager. The effort should be of primary concern to a country whose very economic survival is tied to the problem of preservation of the game herd. Kenya is a beautiful land with staggering geography, but without the attraction of its wild game, tourism would dwindle very quietly to a trickle as it did in Tanzania, where for a long time it was difficult and uncomfortable for the tourist. Recently there has been a change of attitude based, no doubt, on the government of Tanzania recognizing the economic potential of tourism for their country. Uganda destroyed itself through wars and the wild game was virtually eliminated by the automatic weapons of Amin's undisciplined troops. Vigorous attempts are now being made to restore this valuable national treasure to Uganda.

How can a society which cannot even protect its chief economic resource from sure destruction, be expected to surmount the problems of population control and epidemic spread of such a devastating disease as AIDS? Involvement by the West cannot accomplish these goals no matter how well meaning. Only change from within, a change of behavior and attitude, can be expected to have a lasting effect or bring about the changes that are needed now.

It has now been more than four decades since that first trip to Africa. Much has happened in the intervening years. I went back time and again. I still go there. What began with three surgeons and a tiny airplane grew into the largest non-governmental health care organization in Africa, with a permanent staff of over five hundred, a fleet of aircraft, an extensive radio network, a comprehensive training program for health care workers in rural areas and urban slums, and a responsibility to bring health care, public health and educational services to hundreds of thousands of Africans.

All of these programs have been developed with an eye to their usefulness in an African context, and most importantly, are aimed toward the goal of self-reliance. I feel privileged to have played a very small role in this bit of history, but mostly to have had the unique opportunity to work side-by-side with so many dedicated professionals who place the needs of their patients above their own. God bless them all.